W9-AAD-396

# AFTER EFFECTS MOST WANTED

## CHRISTIAN DARKIN
## CHRIS JAMES HEWITT
## JOOST KORNGOLD
## PETER REYNOLDS
## MARK TOWSE
## SIMON TYSZKO

friendsof

DESIGNER TO DESIGNER™

**After Effects Most Wanted**

© 2002 friends of ED

All rights reserved. No part of this book may be reproduced, stored in a retrieval system or transmitted in any form or by any means, without the prior written permission of the publisher, except in the case of brief quotations embodied in critical articles or reviews.

The authors and publisher have made every effort in the preparation of this book to ensure the accuracy of the information. However, the information contained in this book is sold without warranty, either express or implied. Neither the authors, friends of ED nor its dealers or distributors will be held liable for any damages caused or alleged to be caused either directly or indirectly by this book.

First printed October 2002

**Trademark Acknowledgements**

friends of ED has endeavored to provide trademark information about all the companies and products mentioned in this book by the appropriate use of capitals. However, friends of ED cannot guarantee the accuracy of this information.

Published by **friends of ED**
30 – 32 Lincoln Road, Olton, Birmingham,
B27 6PA, UK.

Printed in USA.

**ISBN** 1-904344-02-X

**Authors**
Christian Darkin
Chris James Hewitt
Joost Korngold
Mark Towse
Peter Reynolds
Simon Tyszko

**Editor**
Jon Bounds

**Editorial Proofer**
Dan Britton

**Project Manager**
Jenni Harvey

**Technical Reviewers**
Brian Ganninger
Scott Manning
William McIntyre
Peter Reynolds
Ned Soltz
Kevin Sutherland

**Graphic Editor**
Ty Bhogal

**Cover Design**
Katy Freer
Jon Bounds

**Index**
Simon Collins

**Proof Reader**
Mel Orgee

**Author Agent**
Laura Jones

**Commissioning Editor**
Lums Thevathsan

**Managing Editor**
Sonia Mullineux

**Copyright Thanks to:**
Sony Computer Entertainment Europe Ltd.
The Coca-Cola Company
McDonald's
DDB Sydney

# CONTENTS

# AFTER EFFECTS MOST WANTED

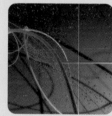

# INTRODUCTION
## Getting the most from this book

How special are your effects? Are you Tim Burton or Ed Wood?

Whether you're working in TV, film, or the Web (or you want to!) you've seen what After Effects *can* do - welcome to the book that'll show you *how* to do it.

We've gathered some of the best and most respected After Effects professionals and got them to reveal what makes them tick - and their FX rock!

At friends of ED we believe we've been the only publisher to take the increase of digital video use seriously, and have substantial experience of publishing on the technology within our DVision books (see www.friendsofED.com/Dvision). Following on from our successful Photoshop Most Wanted, but tailored to the specifics and workflow of After Effects, this book pulls together all of our knowledge and that of our authors into a truly useful package.

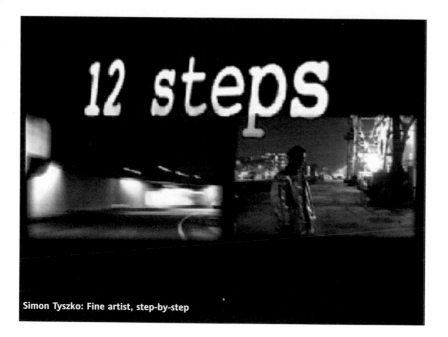

Simon Tyszko: Fine artist, step-by-step

When you look at the work of the authors involved in this book - and at their level it is work, however creative - you can see the true potential of After Effects in the right hands. You may have already seen their work on TV or on the Web - and that's where we hope to see yours, and soon.

Christian Darkin: Bringing prehistoric fish back to life.

This book intends to take your After Effects knowledge and give you a leg-up to the level of our working professionals. It should give you the inspiration to get to the summit and the tools you need to get there - the rest is up to you.

## Layout Conventions

We want this book to be as clear and easy to use as possible, so we've used a number of layout styles throughout.

We'll use different styles to emphasize things like `filenames`, KEYSTROKES OR SHORTCUTS and also hyperlinks.

When we want you to click on a menu, and then through subsequent sub-menus we will indicate to like so: Effect > Blur & Sharpen > Gaussian Blur. This would translate to:

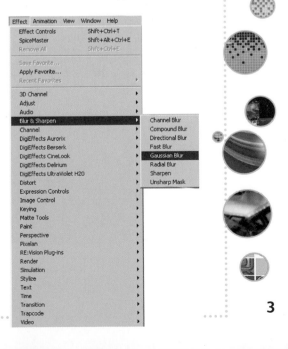

If there's something you should type in then it'll be 'in single quotes'.

1.  Steps that you have to follow will be numbered.

2.  Follow them through, checking the screenshots and diagrams for more hints.

Further explanation of the steps may appear betwixt the steps like so.

3.  When you get to the end, you can stop - and you'll have a finished effect.

## On the CD

As I'm sure you're aware, digital video files are huge and try as we might, there is no way we could fit all of the pre-rendered After Effects Projects onto one CD, Christian Darkin's museum piece, for example was over seven Gig! What we've done is included enough material for each chapter for you to follow and recreate our Most Wanted effects - and where time, space and copyright have allowed us, the final movies. If the final movie file is not in the chapter folder we've included web addresses where they can be found.

The CD content is organized in folders, each titled as the chapter and containing everything you need to follow our authors' instructions. You as readers are encouraged to build your own customized projects.

"Jenovah - Joost Korngold"

## Support – we're here to help

All books from friends of ED aim to be easy to follow and error-free. However, if you do run into problems, don't hesitate to get in touch – our support is fast, friendly and free.

You can reach us at support@friendsofED.com, quoting the last four characters of the ISBN in the subject of the e-mail (that's 402X), and even if our dedicated support team are unable to solve your problem immediately, your queries will be passed onto the people who put the book together, the editors and authors, to solve. All foED authors help with the support on their books, and will either directly mail people with answers, or (more usually) send their response to an editor to pass on.

We'd love to hear from you, even if it's just to request future books, ask about friends of ED, or tell us how much you loved *After Effects Most Wanted*.

To tell us a bit about yourself and make comments about the book, why not fill out the reply card at the back and send it to us.

If your enquiry concerns an issue not directly concerned with book content, then the best place for these types of questions is our message board lists at http://friendsofed.infopop.net/2/OpenTopic. Here, you'll find a variety of designers talking about what they do, who should be able to provide some ideas and solutions.

For news, more books, sample chapters, downloads, author interviews, our new PDF shop and loads more, send your browser to www.friendsofED.com.

Away you go!

# PETER REYNOLDS

Peter started his career in fine arts, but the lure of animation and motion graphics proved to be irresistible (i.e. too much fun!). He is the founder of alkamy studio (www.alkamy.com) which, at times, feels more like a playground than a work place, allowing the fusion of traditional art techniques with the latest in digital thing-a-ma-jigs.

When he can find the time, Peter continues to practice in time-based arts, and strives to bring innovation and fresh ideas into his commercial projects. Peter enjoys the myriad possibilities to create fake realities that come from digital imaging technology and thrives on the challenge of creating an illusion of contiguous space and time that comes with compositing.

Peter leads a very animated life with his wife and studio partner Marie, Kimi the Director of Entertainment & resident samoyed, and his imaginary friend, HAL. Everything is running smoothly. And you?

Self-Portrait 1669
Rembrandt Harmenszoon van Rijn (1606-1669)

The main idea for this television commercial came from the agency DDB Sydney Pty Ltd and the execution of the concept came from the Kotij's Art Director, Mike Seymour. In this case it was a very clearly defined brief, and for me the challenge and inspiration came from the requirement to replicate and simulate the right amount of detail and variety found in the real world within a short time frame (which means forget raytraced renders).

Whenever I am faced with a representational project it is often a good idea to consider the techniques of representational artists such as Vermeer and Rembrandt, particularly for their understanding of light and how it determines and defines our vision of everything we see.

These sorts of considerations were important for this brief as it involved details such as simulating the fine texture of the smooth paint that is applied to a bottle cap during the manufacturing process, which was handled in 3D. As well as the important lighting behavior of shadows and reflections, which were perfected in the 2D composite, all of which are required to 'sell' a shot to an audience and keep your clients happy.

Girl Interrupted at her Music
Johannes Vermeer (1632-1675)

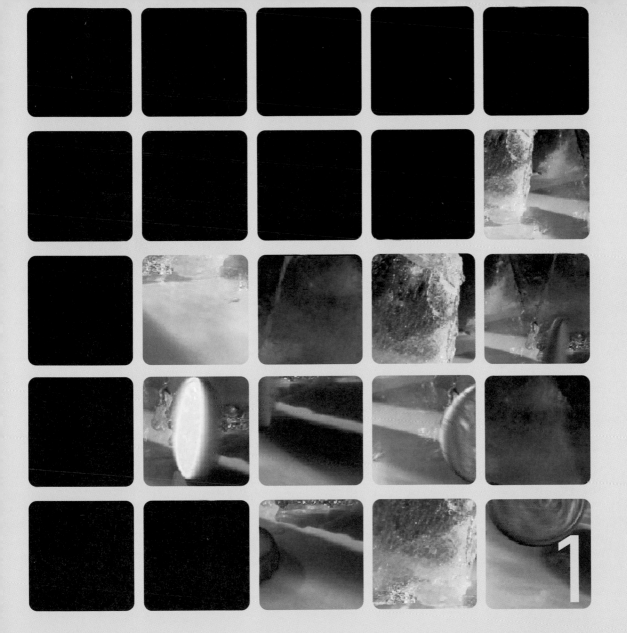

# I'D BUY THAT FOR A DOLLAR
## Reflections, Shadows and 3D

1

In this chapter we will be working through a segment of a television commercial for a one dollar Coca-Cola deal from McDonald's, which I worked on for kotij (www.kotij.com).

The advertising world requires quick turnaround times from media-savvy clients who have a sharp eye for detail and an acute awareness of deadlines. This example involves combining 2D and 3D elements, with a focus on how we can use compositing to achieve great results in the shortest possible time.

We will also see how a desktop compositor such as After Effects remains extremely useful for post-production facilities, even when they have high-end systems such as discreet's flame or inferno compositing systems.

The brief was to make a spinning dollar coin change into a spinning cap to reveal it is a Coca-Cola bottle top.

## Cinéma vérité

Imagine the difficulties of trying to match the coin spin and the cap spin with live action so that the change was convincing. We needed results fast, so we turned to 3D animation and compositing.

For realistic animation it often helps to have some reference footage, and this is the first area where After Effects can keep valuable production time down. We used a DV camera to film a coin spin, so that we didn't have to worry about camera set ups, lock-offs or multiple takes. Then to help interpret the coin motion correctly, we removed the camera movements and shake by tracking the background to steady the shot.

In the Production Bundle of After Effects, there is a Tracker/Stabilizer available to steady shaky shots, open the layer window and you will find it in the layer menu. This tool works by tracking the position of a group of pixels from one frame to the next. You need to pick a point which, in physical reality, was stable, even though the camera shake has it moving all over the place.

Ideal areas to track have the following attributes:

- They remain in shot the whole time.
- They are significantly different from other areas in the frame.
- The shape remains stable.
- The area contains high contrast.
- The area's color remains steady.

Remember - the computer is tracking a cluster of pixels. If the lighting changes dramatically from one frame to the next, even though the object you are tracking remains on screen, the computer won't be able to locate the cluster of pixels because it will have changed color and perhaps shape.

Within 10 minutes we had some good reference footage and could begin to work out how we were going to animate the 3D objects. The benefit of the stabilized footage was immediate. It revealed that the spinning coin travels in an ever decreasing spiral, which was not as obvious with the raw footage.

## Integration

One of the keys to achieving a successful shot is to integrate all the elements correctly. While there are many things that we can fake in the composite, it's better to try and plan the shot in advance so that the different elements you need to composite are correct in the first place. It pays off to match perspective, camera lens, lighting, and so on, right from the start.

The other thing you need to be mindful of when compositing is to not only check how still frames look, but how the whole comp looks in motion. Some images might not look 'right' as a still frame, but when in motion they work.

# Enjoy comp

In this case, we began with a background plate which was approved by the agency at the first production meeting.

1.  Start a new project and create a composition with a duration of 4 seconds (PAL D1/DV, 720 x 576 was the required size and format for my project – you can chose whatever output options suit you).

2.  Import the file `ice_bgplate.jpg` and place it on the timeline.

This background element is the environment our coin and bottle cap need to inhabit. This means we need to use this plate as a reference for how we produce our 3D elements.

I used Maya to model, texture, light and animate both the coin and cap.

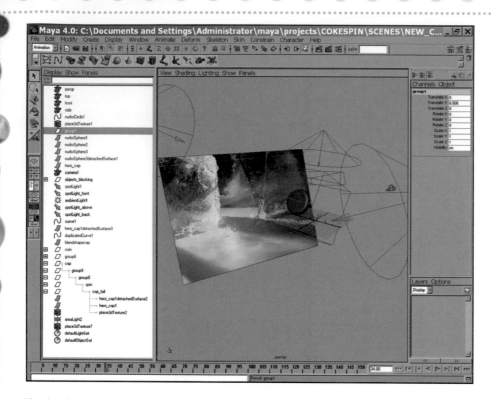

The background plate was taken into Maya, and 3D reference objects were used to 'stand in' for the objects appearing in the 2D plate (ice_bgplate.jpg). The virtual camera was then positioned so that the perspective of the reference objects matched the perspective of the 2D reference plate.

The coin and cap were animated via multiple nodes within Maya. This way I could keyframe different attributes separately, such as spin, rotation, the effect of gravity, and movement along a spiral curve. This made it easier to fine tune the animation or make changes.

The 3D lighting was also adjusted to match the background plate, which was a bit tricky given there were multiple light sources and lots of reflection and refraction going on. All 3D files were rendered with an alpha channel to make it easy for us to composite the various elements.

Once the animation was complete, the 3D scene was rendered in multiple passes, including separate renders for the coin, cap, shadows, and reflections. Rather than rendering all the elements in one pass, this technique allows for more options and flexibility when it comes to the time to make the composite. We can also fake some things in the composite that save us the time and trouble of having to engage in long 3D renders with radiosity effects, etc..

All of the Maya animation was rendered as TIFF sequences.

## Comp this!

Now you know where all these TIFF sequences come from, it's time to start importing them and putting our comp together.

3. Let's begin with the coin. Import the TIFF sequence beginning with `aemw_coin.tif.0001`, and place it above the `ice_bgplate.jpg` layer. Make sure you remember to Show All Files and select the TIFF Sequence option when you import. Unlabelled Alpha should be set to Premultiplied.

4. Now bring in the bottle cap sequence beginning with `aenw_cap.tif.0001`, and place it above the coin layer.

We now need to decide the best time at which the transition from coin to cap should take place. Turn the visibility on and off alternatively for the coin and cap layers and watch the motion of both separately. Then turn them both on and watch the motion combined.

You should notice two important things:

- The coin and cap don't match up exactly.
- The inside of the cap is nice and shiny.

The coin and cap don't match up exactly because when I modeled them in 3D I did it to scale, which means the coin can fit inside the cap. This is important because if we wanted the perfect transition we could match the two elements in 3D exactly. We could even do a 3D morph, matching polygon for polygon. But with the speed at which the objects are traveling and the screen time of the shot, perfectionism in this instance would not pay off, particularly with a tight deadline.

I'm sure you're wondering what is important about the 'nice and shiny' cap? It's important because I really like the look of it, so I want to show it off. But the aim here is to benefit the whole shot, which means I can't let the fact that I love the way it looks impact my decision on when the transition between the coin and cap should take place. These are just some of the terrible sacrifices, dangers and compromises you are forced to endure, particularly if you are working on the 3D as well as the compositing.

## The transition point

We need to remember that this is the opening shot for the commercial, so the viewer needs some time to register that they are watching a spinning coin, otherwise the change into a Coca-Cola cap loses its significance.

A nice transition point occurs just after the 1 second mark, which gives viewers enough time to register the coin, and also happens to coincide with the point at which gravity begins to change the spin. This speeds up the motion and also puts the coin and cap at an angle which allows for a smoother transition.

**5.** Now let's keyframe the transition, for the cap layer:

1. Move the timeline to 0:00:01:06 and set a keyframe of 0% Opacity.
2. Move the timeline to 0:00:01:07 and set a keyframe of 10% Opacity.
3. Move the timeline to 0:00:01:17 and set a keyframe of 100% Opacity.

**6.** And, for the coin layer:

1. Move the timeline to 0:00:01:12 and set a keyframe of 100% Opacity.
2. Move the timeline to 0:00:01:20 and set a keyframe of 0% Opacity.

The coin and cap have the right perspective for the shot, but, without some reflections and shadows, they still don't look like they're *in* the shot .

## Reflections

**7.** For the reflections off the ice ground plane, bring in the TIFF sequences for the coin and cap, starting with the files `aemw_coin_reflect.tif.0001` and `aemw_cap_reflect.tif.0001`.

**8.** Put the new reflection layers on the timeline.

**9.** Select the coin reflection layer and set the Transfer Mode to Lighten (Layer > Transfer Mode > Lighten). At `0:00:01:12`, set Opacity to 60% and on the next frame, `0:00:01:13`, set Opacity to 0%.

**10.** Select the cap reflection layer and set the Transfer Mode to Screen. At `0:00:01:09` set Opacity to 0%. At `0:00:01:16` set Opacity to 49%.

**11.** For both reflection layers, add a Gaussian Blur of 1.0.

## And now for something completely subtle

You will note that the reflections are fairly subtle so as to not pull the eye away from the main action. Now let's add more detail that's completely fake, and even more subtle, but helps sell the shot.

We are going to add reflections in the blocks of ice, behind the main action. This is a quick trick, but that's fine because we don't want to bring attention to it, we just want it as set dressing.

12. Duplicate the coin layer 3 times.

13. There are 3 sections of ice on the right of the background plate. Position the 3 duplicate layers on the 3 respective sections of ice.

14. Using the Pen tool, create a mask for each layer that somewhat reflects the shape of the ice sections.

15. Adjust Opacity for each of the masked layers to reflect depth and distance from the foreground:

- Mask 1 = 15%
- Mask 2 = 10%
- Mask 3 = 7%

16. Manipulate the timeline duration for these layers so that the reflection in each section of ice only shows up when the coin is near it:

Now play around with effects such as Texturize, Fast Blur and Blend to really go for that subtle feeling.

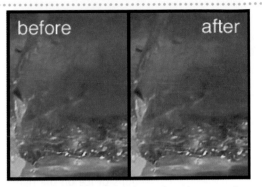

To do the same thing for the block of ice on the left side, duplicate the cap layer, mask it, and make sure the reflection only shows up when the cap comes near it. Because it's red, it's a bit more obvious, so although it's closer to camera, I made the opacity 12% for this one. Another important note is to make sure the time for this layer is slightly out of phase with the time for the original cap layer so that the reflection appears to mirror the cap layer. I also used the Texturize, Fast Blur and Ripple effects for the cap reflection.

## The shadow

Our coin and cap are starting to look like they're in the shot, but there's nothing that places an object in a scene quicker than a good shadow or two.

To save an eternity in a 3D program, perfecting radiosity and raytraced shadows, basic shadows were rendered instead. These shadows can now be manipulated in the composite to give a greater sense of realism.

There's a lot of light bouncing around and reflecting off surfaces in our background plate. Rather than having a distinct and sharp edged shadow, we're going to smooth the edges off and also reduce the shadow intensity as it moves away from the coin and cap.

17.  Import the shadow TIFF sequences for the coin and cap and bring them onto the timeline:

```
aemw_coin_shadow.tif.0001
aemw_cap_shad.tif.0001
```

18.  Add Opacity keyframes to both layers so that the coin shadow vanishes and the cap shadow appears as the coin changes to the cap.

19.  Add a Gaussian Blur of 70 to both layers (Effect > Blur & Sharpen > Gaussian Blur).

20.  Duplicate the coin and cap shadow layers.

21.  For the duplicate coin layer, add a mask that will roughly divide the moving shadow in half for each frame. Try and make the mask divide the moving shadow in a way that is consistent with the perspective of the shadow. Observe the motion of the coin shadow and then plot the mask. Make adjustments as needed. If you want to get really particular, you could animate the mask, although the shot doesn't really need it.

**22.** Set the Mask Feather to 81 pixels so that our shadows meld. Now reduce the Gaussian Blur for this layer to 15.

**23.** For the duplicate cap layer, add a mask similar to the mask that was added to the duplicate coin layer. Set the Mask Feather to 81 pixels and bring the Gaussian Blur for this layer down from 70 to 5 so we can see the edges of the bottle cap shadow.

The other thing that helps put the cap in shot is the shadow that falls across the far edge of the cap. This shadow was done in 3D to match the strong stripe of shadow in the background plate.

## Almost there...

The shadows are starting to look nice. Although there is a lot of light reflecting around the scene, even off the ground, as the cap comes to rest it will probably look more convincing with a darker shadow directly beneath it. Now to just take it that little bit further we turn to Photoshop.

**24.** Move the timeline to the end of the comp after the cap has come to rest. Anywhere after `0:00:03:15` should be fine. Save the frame as a Photoshop file (Composition > Save Frame As > File). I called this file 'darkside.psd'.

**25.** In Photoshop open up the darkside.psd file. Create a new layer and with the Soft edged Brush tool, paint a dark shadow that we can use directly under the bottle cap. To make it easier to see what you are doing when you paint, you can desaturate the background layer and invert it. You can paint more than one shadow for extra flexibility in the composite. Save your file.

If you haven't got Photoshop, or just want to get on with the tutorial, you can open `darkside.psd` from the CD and use the two shadows that I've created.

**26.** Import the new shadow layer(s) into our After Effects comp.

Play with the shadow opacity until it looks right and then keyframe the Opacity so that the extra shadow appears just as the cap is coming to rest.

## Midas touch

Finally, the agency also requested that the coin look like a new coin. This made me a little nervous at first because the first thing I try and do to remove a 3D CG feel is to dirty objects up with gritty textures. But the agency wanted this one clean and new.

**27.** So to give the coin a little bit of an extra glow at the start, I rendered off a very bright version, which you can load up as a TIFF sequence (`aemw_coin_glow.tif.0001`).

Now let's give that coin a little bit of a twinkle.

**28.** Bring the glow sequence onto its own layer, making sure it is above the coin layer, etc.. Set the Opacity of the glow layer to 13%.

**29.** Now, with the Opacity attribute selected, add an expression (Animation > Add Expression). Add the expression: `opacity.wiggle(25,5,3,1)`.

Because our composition is 25 fps, the expression will calculate a new opacity for this layer every frame and will fluctuate/deviate by 5%.

In effect, the glow on the coin will change from frame to frame. Again, like many of the other subtle elements we have added, we probably won't register this consciously when we look at it, but subconsciously it will help sell the shot. Our coin is looking newer already. Mmmmmm... shiny.

## Give me just a little more time

Finally, for all of the elements that need to stay on stage that little bit longer, up to the 4 second mark, such as the cap and its shadows:

**30.** Select the relevant layer, choose Layer > Enable Time Remapping. Now on the timeline, drag the end of the duration bar to the 4 second mark.

The final stacking of your timeline should look something like this:

# Production notes

Often we think fast results and high quality work are mutually exclusive objectives. Yet clients often want both, which is one of the reasons why so many post-production facilities and effects studios make great use of high-end, high-investment compositing systems such as discreet's flame or inferno for commercials. It wouldn't go down well with clients if they asked for a small change and you had to turn to them and say, "Sure, come back next week when it's finished rendering".

The final composite of this commercial was done in kotij's HD inferno suite. So where does After Effects fit in with this? inferno suites are nearly always busy, so it's important to use them for the most crucial steps in the production process, which is usually when you are finishing off a comp with the director or ad agency sitting on your shoulder.

In the meantime it's very handy to have less expensive desktop compositors, such as After Effects, to fall back on, which can be used for client approvals of quick comps along the way. This is exactly what I used After Effects for in this case: to quickly put together a rough comp for initial client approval (which are the files I have enclosed on the CD).

Another excellent option in that regard is discreet's combustion 2, which is naturally well positioned to be passing comp files into inferno. A demo version can be found at: www.discreet.com/products/combustion/

If you're interested in the wider world of compositing, or perhaps have ambitions that lean toward Inferno, then combustion 2 is a great place to start.

So now you should have a good idea of how to integrate 3D and 2D into a comp, as well as how much time you can save by continually breaking down shots into manageable and customizable elements.

You should also have an insight into how After Effects can be used in a very busy production environment. Compositing can really save you time, particularly if you haven't got all day to wait for those perfectly rendered radiosity lighting and shadows.

## Credits

A special thanks goes to Mike Seymour, a highly gifted compositor and art director, and a great guy to work with. Mike is always generous with his vast knowledge of effects, which he shares world wide as one of the founders of the excellent compositing information site: www.fxguide.com.

Client: McDonald's
Agency: DDB Sydney Pty Ltd
Studio: kotij (www.kotij.com)
Producer: Prue Fletcher
Creative Director: Mike Seymour
Final Composite (Inferno Artist): Mark Vandenbergen
Initial Composite (After Effects): Peter Reynolds
3D: Peter Reynolds
Composite for After Effects Most Wanted: Peter Reynolds

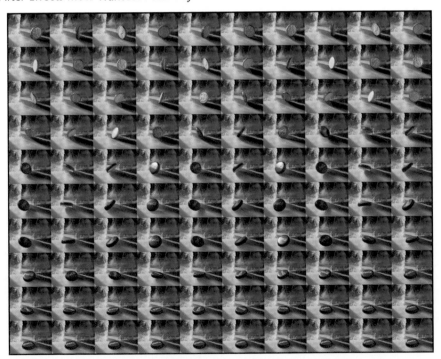

A DDB Sydney commercial, for McDonald's Australia. Copyright 2002, All rights reserved

# MARK TOWSE

Mark Towse is the founder and managing director of Bigimpact TV Ltd, formed in April 2000. Bigimpact specializes in both Internet design, and TV and film post-production. Mark also regularly writes for magazines and is, in particular, one of the UK's top After Effects specialists. He writes regular articles and tutorials on all things After Effects and DV related, including cover features, for the likes of Computer Arts, Computer Arts Specials, DV World, Mac Format, Create Online and Digit.

Despite new media being his driving passion, Mark has ventured into and specialized in many fields – including computer games, even having been the UK National Computer Games Champion, for 94, 95 and 96. Despite numerous appearances on the small screen (If you tot up all the appearances on 17 different shows at one time or another, he has been seen by a gargantuan 30 million + people!), Mark is keen to emphasize how much cooler motion graphics are than 15 minutes.

"I studied at Loughborough university in, of all things, Economics and Accountancy before seeing the light.

I did a 'proper' academic subject and hated every minute of it. I started working with Photoshop on the Student magazine before getting hooked and deciding that after University, I would become a master of all things digital art related.

I had experimented in various types of motion graphics with Flash and Director, but you'd hardly class them as production quality animation tools. When I discovered After Effects, at its very green version 2 stage, I was hooked. I learnt it inside out and have never looked back."

Now married to a Czech artist, named Marketa, Mark is also working with some UK terrestrial TV networks on some innovative new program ideas, along with fronting the new digital imagery company Digital Divas."

You can check out the Bigimpact TV web site at www.bigimpact.tv.

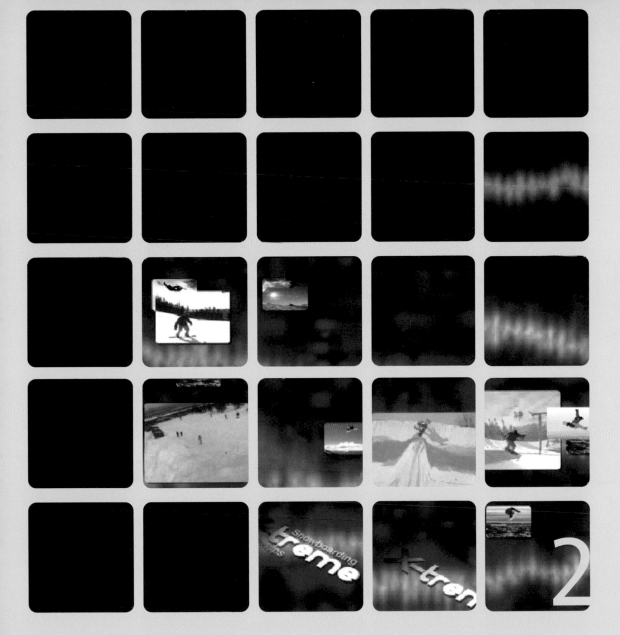

EXTREME FX
Multiple video clips and Morphing

2

Bigimpact TV is a small new media design agency based just outside London, in the Thames 'Silicon Valley'. We were approached to create an intro sequence for a TV production company who were making a few shows about the European Snowboarding Championships 2000. We were asked to make the sequence very 'MTV style', so lots of movement, lots of excitement and – here's the stinker – it had to be 52 seconds long. Not normally a problem, but how the hell do you keep a section interesting for 52 seconds without showing a load of snowboarders doing tricks? Not that showing a load of snowboarders doing tricks wouldn't be interesting, but wouldn't that just be a little bit predictable?

## The brief

It's quite tricky when you are faced with a project that gives you a heap of creative freedom, but unfortunately – more often than not – the creative choices of such projects are incredibly limited. It's a snowboarding championship. Okay, it has to feature snowboarders. It has to have music in the background and probably something light, given all the snow. Complete cliché, and we didn't want to go for that. Given this, we wanted to make sure the intro we were going to create was different, nay, spectacular! The only thing that we genuinely couldn't avoid using was snowboarders. After all, it was for a snowboarding championship! However, snowboarders always look cool, dynamic and are generally doing something suitably crazy – so this wasn't a problem.

All in all, we were really proud of this project – it took something with the prime potential for mediocrity and transformed it in to a living, breathing piece of audio visual excellence – even if I do say so myself!

We are going to recreate an almost identical version, but we're using different footage, different colors and an ever so slightly different name to the original, the X-treme Snowboarding Championships rather than 'European'. We'll be dumping the stroke effect for spelling European and using something slightly more suitable for the X-treme nature of our clip.

The concepts and techniques we will be using in this chapter are all identical to what we did in 2000, when we were commissioned for the project. However, as technology progresses so does our ability to do cool stuff, so sporadically we will be using some of After Effects enhanced features, which I will point out along the way.

Again, due to copyright laws, we will be using different clips of snowboarders doing their thing, as well as a different, but equally suitable, soundtrack. You wouldn't believe the amount of legal etiquette that has to be gone through when a company sub-contracts work to you for a large TV network and you try to republish what you have actually done. Let this, in itself, be a cautionary tale. If you can arrange it, it is always good to be able to sign a clause in your contract stating that you also have the rights to publish your work for the sole purpose of your own promotion. You won't always be in a position to be able to do this, especially if the main TV network client isn't aware that the people who won their contract are subsequently subbing out a lot of the work.

Right then – let's get our hands dirty!

## Building the background

Look and feel-wise, we really didn't want fading clips on a snow-white background, as you might see on Winter Olympics coverage and the like. We wanted to do on the screen what snowboarding had done on the slopes – add a different atmosphere and style. With this in mind, we were thinking that we could use smaller clips over an organic background with constant 'brooding' motion; the feeling that there was something living and breathing behind the boarders' death-defying feats. We decided in the end to make it dark and moody, which actually ended up emphasizing the lightness of the clips that we were using of the snowboarders in the foreground. However, a dark moody background could do with something to give it that special spark.

Different companies work in different ways, but we like to build from the absolute basics, through to the more advanced features. There are a number of benefits to this. Backgrounds which run through the bulk of animations take a relatively small amount of time to render, and doing so will enable you to see the more advanced elements of the animation as they will appear against them. With this in mind, we are starting with our morphing background.

1.    Create a new composition (size should be 720 by 576 for UK Pal, which is the standard resolution of the UK Pal standard, or 720 by 486 - the standard specifications for the NTSC format), called 'Background'. Make it 10.01 seconds long, with 25 frames per second (or 29.97 for NTSC areas).

2.    Create a new solid  (Layer > New > Solid) the same size as the composition, and call it 'Colors'. From the Effect menu, pick Render > 4-Color Gradient.

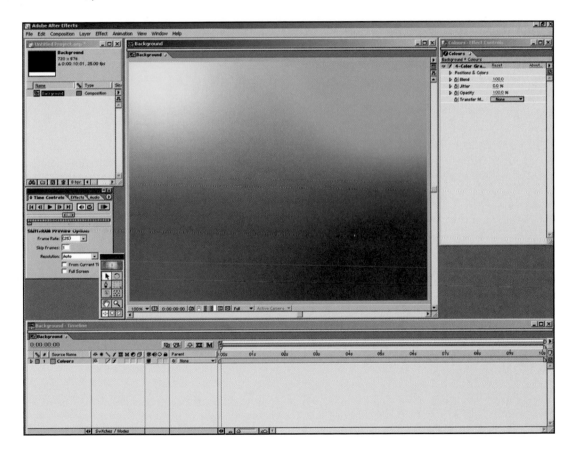

3. Expand the Position & Colors attribute within the Effects window, then click on each of the colors and change them to a different shade of blue. Increase the Blend setting to about 150 to increase the subtlety of the blues merging.

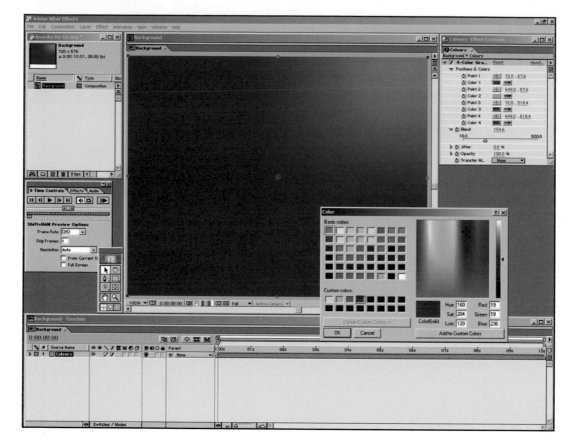

4. Create another solid, this time called 'Organic'. From the Effects menu, select Fractal Noise, the excellent ex-Cult Effects filter 'Noise Turbulent'. You will get a nice swirl of fractals. All well and good, but not really the feel we're after. Change the Fractal Type to Max and the Noise Type to Soft linear. This gives a nice kind of blobby appearance.

Feel free to experiment with other fractal types. We chose Max as it was the most subdued and least erratic – nice and smooth. This is one of the fractal types that doesn't require much assistance to make it look good. Also, the complexity settings are all null after 4; we decided to take out the miniature blobs by changing complexity to 2. It isn't recommended that you keyframe this setting, as the appearance of blobs is instant, rather than smooth.

5. On the timeline, drag the Organic layer below the Colors layer, so that it is obscured. We now want to mix the two together using blending modes. At the bottom of the timeline, you will see a bar saying Switches/Modes. Click on this text and you can swap between the two main control areas of After Effects. When you are on the modes section (the one with drop-down boxes saying Normal), click on the Colors layer and select Multiply.

Again, feel free to experiment, but this setting gave us the subtlest look. We could have selected a different mode and changed the Fractal Noise effect's brightness and contrast settings to achieve the same. Our way is easier to implement, but not to be used if you require a higher degree of control. The easy way is best – under these circumstances.

6.   Click on the Organic layer and press E. This is a shortcut which toggles between viewing and hiding the Effect properties for the layer selected. Expand the options – there are several more in this newly updated version of the effect, which can be awkward if you are working on a smaller monitor.

We are going to animate the Evolution parameter that animates the blobs in the background. We want this to cycle every 10 seconds, which is a long enough duration to prevent the audience from recognizing that the scene is repeating, without needing to render and animate parameters over the full 52 second duration of the final composition.

7.   Create a keyframe (click the small stopwatch), then select the layer and press U.

This is the one of the most useful shortcuts in After Effects. It hides all settings apart from those that have keyframes. Now we have no clutter in the timeline and can organize better.

**8.** Move the timeline head to the end of the composition, the ten-second point, and create another keyframe. Now, on this second keyframe, select one full evolution.

You will see the screen change, as – perversely – one complete evolution doesn't return the blobs to their starting position. There are new settings we can use to avoid any problems.

**9.** Expand the Evolution Options in the Effect Controls window, and turn on Cycle Evolution. Set Cycle (in revolutions) to 1. This will cycle back to the starting position for every complete evolution. Ours is – of course – at ten seconds.

Finally, for the background, we want to return to the 4-Color Gradient filter on the Colors layer, animate the positions of the colors, and alter the colors themselves.

**10.** Keyframe at the start, middle and end for each of the colors and the color positions, and animate as you see fit. To ensure the color changes loop smoothly, keyframe the starting position, then keyframe around the middle of the timeline, and finally copy the starting keyframe and paste it as the end keyframe. That way the keyframes will end where they started.

**11.** Render the background (Composition > Add To Render Queue). Keep the default settings, or if your machine is lacking power, render as an AVI file with the Indio video 5.10 codec at 100% quality, which will give you a much more manageable file size with no noticeable loss of quality.

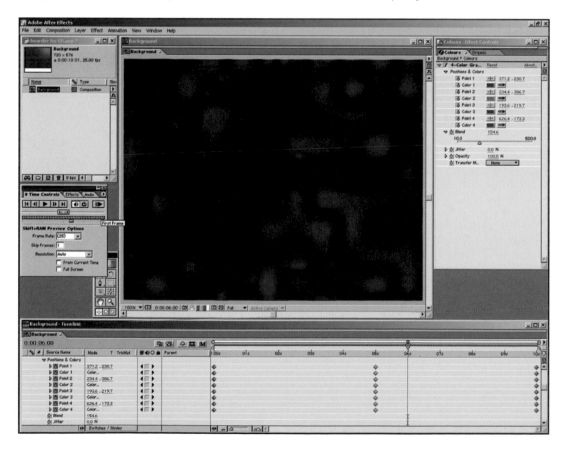

# We are waving

We knew that we were going to have to have a funky soundtrack, but we weren't sure whether or not it would be something like jazz-funk or electronica – both would be quite suitable. In the end we plumped for a track that one of our DJ friends had been mixing, which the lovely lad let us have the rights to use – a fairly hard slab of techno. Given that, we figured the background couldn't just be animated, it had to go with the music and really make the screen come to life. Everyone has seen the analog lines or dots pumping to the music in some clip or other, but what could we do that would really make things start jumping? We figured that if we blended one of the analog line settings in the audio waveform with the background, and applied a lot of blurs, glows and the like, then we could change the feeble audio waveform into something really special, and we did! It actually ended up making the background look a million more times impressive than the level of complexity deserved, but it did the trick and that kept me happy into the wee hours.

**12.** Create a new composition the same size as before, call it 'Main Comp B', and make it 52 seconds long. Import the AVI file of the background you've just created. When the video file is in the project organization palette, select it and choose from the File menu, Interpret Footage > Main. Change the number of times the clip loops to 6, change the Pixel Aspect Ratio to Square Pixels.

Because Indeo Video is a video codec, it automatically assumes a TV aspect ratio – great for our final render, but it distorts our work by stretching it horizontally in the meantime. This Interpret Footage command removes any such distortions, and will instantly enlarge the length of the clip on the timeline.

**13.** In the timeline, grab the small gray handle at the end of the background clip and drag it to the end of the timeline.

We now want to create our funky beating audio waveform, which is going to really jazz up the proceedings.

**14.** Import the file `HornyScratch.wav` from the CD and drag the audio file to the timeline. Perform the same Interpret Footage command on the WAV file as you did for `background.avi`.

**15.** Create another solid, called 'Audio Waveform', and apply the Audio Waveform filter to the solid (Effect > Render > Audio Waveform). In the Effect Controls panel, change the Audio Layer to the `HornyScratch.wav` layer, and you will see the filter kick in.

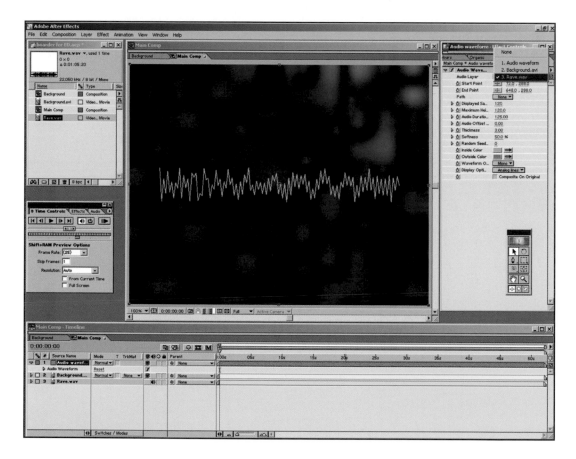

**16.** Now for the touches that make this project great. Set the start and the end points of the waveform to the left and right edges of the screen. Now change the Inside Color to white, and the Outside Color to a vivid blue (0,0,255 RGB). Now increase the Thickness setting of the filter to 91, Softness to 100%, and Displayed Samples to 24 (everything is too squashed at higher levels for the effect we are trying to achieve). Increase the Maximum Height of the samples to 184.

**17.** We have used the offset audio sample setting, as the very first fraction of the sample is quiet and thus makes the effect flat-line. The offset command delays the graphical representation of the audio waveform, preventing any boring flatness in the effect, even for a split second! Set the audio offset to one second, as this is where the audio waveform is part way through its initial cycle, and means the graphical representation of the audio offshoot will already be moving when the animation begins.

**18.** Now set the Display Option to Digital – isn't everything looking a lot nicer all of a sudden?

**19.** Now to add some of the finer points. We want to add a Directional Blur filter, from the Blur & Sharpen menu in the Effects section. Use the default 0 degrees settings, but make the blur size 62. Now in the Blending Modes section, select Add. We use this so that the blue halo is multiplied with the background to create a lighter glowing halo, which merges with the background. Make sure the Audio Waveform layer is selected in the timeline and press T to open the Opacity controls. Set the Opacity to 60. Now for the touch of genius.

**20.** Copy and paste the Audio Waveform layer. On the new layer delete the Directional Blur. Press E to open the Effects controls and modify the settings as follows: reduce Maximum Height from 184 to 124, change Thickness to 90, the display to Analog Lines, and change the Displayed Samples to 84. Change Opacity to 40, and now things are really starting to take shape.

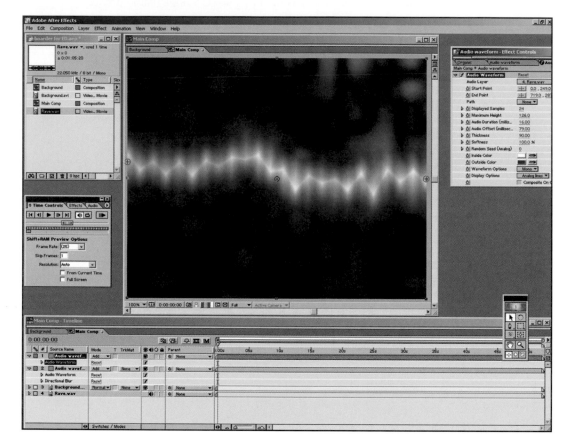

If you do a test RAM preview now, you will see the waveforms going crazy. Don't worry – we planned to pre-compose and time stretch this later, as we move and animate the waveform comps depending on the needs provided by our morphing snowboarder clips. We will also be using multiple instances of these waveforms, with various transformations attached. For now, turn off the audio waveform layers by clicking on the small eyeball button in the timeline, to the left or right (depending on your default settings) of the layer name.

## Footage IN

With a good solid base for the intro sequence, we had to work out how to make the boarders more interesting – for the sake of our animators rather than the viewers! I'd been playing around with a fun new plug-in from Re:Vision Effects (www.revisionfx.com), the excellent Re:Flex Morph, which lets you morph not just between images by using masks, but also morph moving footage. This is particularly rare outside 3D packages, and I had some useful results with a few test renders of some friends morphing as they were running along.

Given that the plug-in works particularly well with images with clearly defined edges and a good solid central focal point, my mind started turning towards how we could be using this for our snowboarding footage, which was even more perfect for the task. Given the bright threads and generally white backgrounds it would be fairly easy to have boarders leaping to monstrous heights and, at the zenith of their feats morphing, into the start of another trick (or indeed, into another boarder who was finishing their previous feat!) – smart.

Of course, it didn't turn out to be quite that easy, but the concept was cool, and was definitely going into the project. Stylistically, there wasn't much more to decide with regards to our boarder clips, as we already had something fairly unique and very cool to put on the screen. However, with several clips bombing around the screen at any one time, it was always going to be too busy. I'd seen a really good idea on, of all places, a morning chat show. They had clips of various celebrity guests scrolling along the screen in a line at the top. Occasionally one would shoot into the center of the screen, enlarging rapidly for a few seconds before shooting back into the scrolling line. Good graphics on morning TV, what will they think of next? This set my idea muscle flexing uncontrollably.

We had one problem with the boarding clips: we didn't have a huge number of them to work with at the time and the really interesting part of the clip, from start of jump or trick to landing, is just a few seconds, if that. We solved this by keeping the first frame of clips static until we had them enlarging on the screen, which menat that we had to use fewer clips. It would be great for the viewers to see something about to happen, speculate, and rapidly see the stunts, which then transform into other stunts.

It was at this point that we decided to desaturate all the clips whilst they were static and small, to make sure that the viewers eyes weren't getting distracted at any time from the main point of the action. Of course, it was unlikely that they would, but to check this out we tried a mini render (having already put together some of the fundamental elements at this point). Sure enough, we had been right in assuming that some of the very colorful clips were really distracting when put against their more somberly tinted counterparts. We color corrected the desaturated images, as more often than not an image which has had all of its color removed simply doesn't look very good – more pastel shades being a prime example of this. Remove the color and you have a scene full of gray, which merges and removes too much detail, so we also corrected brightness and contrast (actually using some of the more fully featured Boris plug-ins, which should be part of every pro's arsenal – but the standard AE color correcting, brightness and contrast controls are just as useful for most situations), which made the desaturated images look perfect on our moody background. With some keyframed color correction on the enlarged images, the piece was starting to take shape nicely.

We decided to make the clips travel across the screen in various straight lines. They would enlarge (always with the top left hand corner as the anchor point), do their funky thing, shrink, and then travel off in another direction at 90 degrees. The direction would depend on the initial movement of the clip. Just for some extra funkiness, we decided to have a glowing edge to the clips and to round off their corners. There was no special reason for this – it already looked great. However, if you want to look that deep into the project, you could say snowboarders are more curved edge types than straight lines – leave those to their arch nemeses, the skiers!

Now's the part you've all been waiting for – animating the static images and morphing the clips. Be warned. This isn't easy, but is definitely worth the perseverance.

21. In the project window, we need to organize our assets, as things are about to get a bit crowded otherwise. Click the mini folder icon four times, and rename the folders as 'Statics', 'Clips', 'Elements' and 'Compositions'. You must now move the comps to the compositions folder, etc. Next, import the static images to the Statics folder from the CD-ROM, and the clips to the Clips folder.

**22.** Drag `static_1.tif` to the timeline. I have taken the liberty of adding an alpha channel in Photoshop to curve the edges. This is much easier than fiddling around trying to draw equal curved masks on each edge. Just use the Guess alpha channel when prompted.

**23.** Use the filter Effects > Image Control > Tint. Some of the Boris filters are far superior for all kinds of color correction, but this will do if you haven't got access to them. For this effect, simply slide up the Amount to Tint setting to 100%.

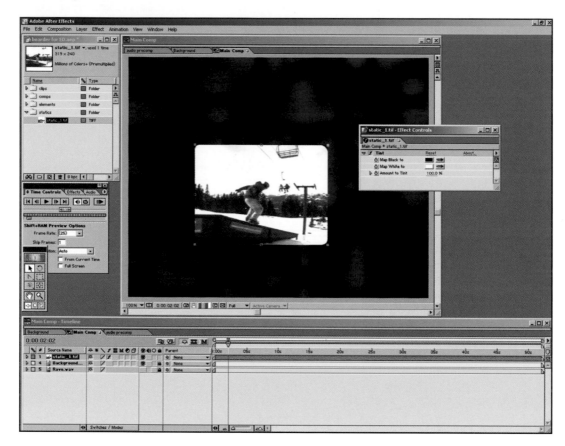

**24.** Our static image now needs shrinking and animating. We're going to start by selecting the static_1.tif layer, pressing S and shrinking the image to 40% of its original size.

**25.** Now is the time to turn on the action and title safe areas, to make sure all your action can be viewed on even the pokiest TV screens. In the main comp screen window, you will see a sort of crosshairs icon next to the 100% screen size drop-down. Click this and you will be shown the title and action safe areas of the screen.

All of our main action needs to take place within the action safe region, although I always err on the side of caution as small 14in TVs lose a greater proportion of the final picture than conventional safe areas suggest.

**26.** Position our shrunken static image to just underneath the bottom of the screen, and to the right of the title safe area.

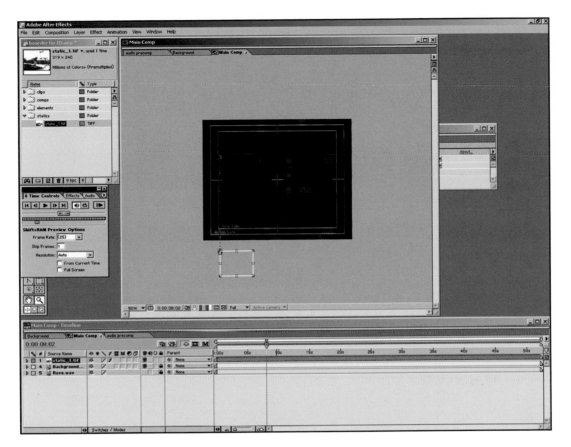

**27.** Time to start animating, so select the static_1.tif layer and press P to access the positional controls. Place a keyframe in the timeline at eight seconds, as we are later going to use the first five seconds to bring in the music, fade up the background and start the audio waveform bouncing around the screen. Place another keyframe at nine seconds and move the image up to near the top of the screen.

Now we change the anchor point so that when we scale, it will scale not from the center but from the relevant edge. We want it to scale towards the center from the top left.

**28.** Set the anchor point by selecting the layer and pressing A. Set to x = 0 and y = 0. You can adjust the positional settings again now to take into account the anchor point alteration. Yes, we could have done this at the start, but even most hardened AE users are so unused to altering anchor points that I thought it would be useful to see it in action.

**29.** Now add a scale keyframe at 9 seconds and one at 10 seconds, changing the scale to 100% at 10 seconds. Bring up the Tint option and keyframe at 9 and 10 seconds, changing the 100% amount of Tint value to 0% at 10 seconds.

This means that as the static is increasing in size, the color is returning to the image, which looks nice.

**30.** Now, select the layer, press U to open up all elements with keyframes, and select all the keyframes by click-dragging with your mouse. Now go to Animation > Keyframe Assistant > Easy Ease to nicely remove the linear feel and make the animation a bit more 'curved', like the pulsing background.

**31.** Drag the small gray layer handle at the end of the static_1.tif layer to the 10-second mark.

**32.** This means after 10 seconds, the image will no longer be visible. This is the point at which we replace the image with the clip.

**33.** Drag the clip onto the timeline and position it on the screen at the same location as the static image. Make sure it is lined up directly after the image ends on the timeline. You may find it easier to position the clip by changing its opacity, placing it over the top of the static, and then increasing Opacity back to 100%.

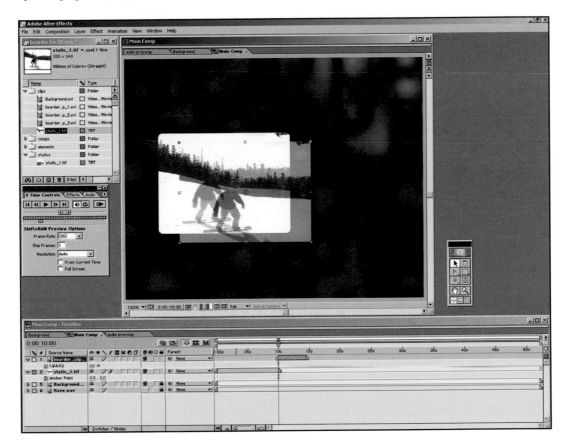

**34.** Now you can drag the static_1_end.tif file, which is a static image of the final frame of the clip, to the timeline. Repeat the anchor point steps and shrink from 100% to 40% as before, keyframing the tint as well.

**35.** Now create position keyframes, and this time make the static shoot off to the right hand side of the screen. Don't forget to 'relax' things with the keyframe assistant's Easy Ease function. These are the basics of what is going to happen throughout the initial section of the intro animation. When the clip ends and the new static starts to shrink, a new static shoots on to the screen from the other side and carries on in similar style.

Don't worry, we haven't forgotten the morphing. We're just making sure you had all the concepts before we get to the real nitty-gritty.

**36.** Press CTRL + Z a few times (undo) to get to just before we introduced the second static image. Now move the timeline head to just where our boarder dude is raising his arms. Pause there. This is the point of the first clip at which we want to morph into another trick.

Make sure you have installed the demo version of the Re:Flex Warp plug-in. Re:Flex morph is used for morphing static images, whereas some tricks and cross dissolving allow us to sneakily morph moving clips together. The supplied help files are a little confusing for the novice, so you'll find the steps covered here to get you started.

37. Drag the clip, boarder_clip_3.avi, onto the timeline so that the clip starts at the same point as where the boarder in the first clip raises his arms backwards. Make sure the new clip is aligned directly over the top of the first clip, and make it invisible with the eyeball icon.

38. Now select the first clip and use the Re:Flex Warp filter (it should appear at Effects > RE:Vision Plug-ins > RE:Flex Warp – if it doesn't check your installation).

## Morph

What we are actually going to do is warp, over time, the boarder from the first clip into the position of the boarder in the second clip. We then warp the boarder in the second clip to the shape of the boarder in the first clip, and then cross dissolve the two for a perfect morph.

1. The filter works with masks. You draw a mask 'geometry' on the first boarder, let's say, the shape of the back contour of the boarder's leg. Then, on the same frame, we keep the first layer selected (so its masks are visible), but turn on the visibility of the second clip, so we can draw a new mask on the first clip, using the second clip as a guide/tracing layer. Then when you turn the second clip's visibility back off, you have the first mask being the 'warp from' mask, and the filter automatically uses the second mask as the 'warp to' mask. Then, we need to create subsequent masks (one for the head, board, front of leg contour, individual arms, torso, etc.) until after about a second's worth of frames.

When you draw the second mask you will see the filter warp the entire clip to an extent. To prevent any distortions while you are placing all the relevant geometries, you should turn off (but not remove!) the filter by clicking on the *f* at the top of the Effects Controls box for the RE:Flex Warp filter.

2. Now continue to create from and to masks on the clip 1, making sure that the clip 1 layer is always selected, even when you turn on the visibility for clip 2, to see where you should place the 'to' masks. Don't use closed masks, as they will operate like normal masks and create a matte, removing a big chunk of the visible picture.

3. This screenshot shows the to and from masks on clip 1, with both visibilities turned off – you get the idea now? In full, I created 7 'from' and 7 'to' masks, meaning 14 masks. We need to animate these masks. First, click M to open the mask options, and click on alternate mask's color boxes, and change the 'to' masks to color red, so you can see the difference.

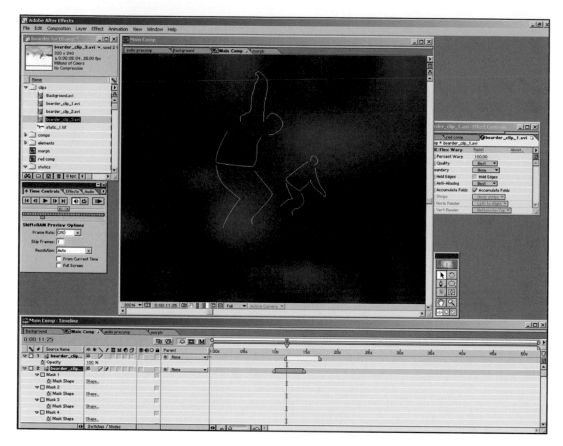

4. Now, here comes the real slog. We have to animate the masks for each, yes *each* frame – this is why I only wanted to make a 1 second warp between the 2 clips. If we're doing 5 or 6 clip morphs, you're going to be animating quite a lot of masks.

A 1-second morph is over 100 individual animations, but 2-second morphs would literally have to double that. It is possible to just keep the masks as they are. The warp will still take place, but it won't look like it can do – and quality counts if you want a second commission.

5. The way we do this mammoth task is by creating individual keyframes in the Mask Shape control in the timeline. I have created keyframes at the start of the clip and at the place we want the morph to begin. Then you must create 25 keyframes, 1 per frame (or the equivalent for NTSC users) and keyframe each mask at each frame, manipulating the masks so the 'from' masks change each frame 'to' match the first boarder, and the 'to' masks change to match the second boarder if your using NTSC, which you can again check by turning on and off visibility.

Using your own judgment, you can reduce some workload by keyframing every two frames, rather than each individual frame. Well then, best get to it – see you on the other side...

Now, you can add a boundary, which limits the area that is affected by a warp, so when you turn on the effect, you won't see the outer edge of the clip distorted.

6. With four lines almost make a complete box inside the edge of the clip – don't forget to not close the masked box. Then rename the new mask as 'Boundary' and move it to the bottom of the mask stack. Now, in the Effect Controls, select the Boundary mask as the boundary. This must be at the bottom, so the filter does not use the box to interpolate any of the mask warps. The next step is to set Opacity to 100%, with a keyframe at the end of the mask warps set to 0. Make keyframes in the Effect Controls for the percentage of warp completion; set 0% at the first keyframe and 100% at the second keyframe. Now if you turn on the effect and do a RAM preview, goodness gracious me – the first boarder only morphs into the second boarder.

However, you will see the 'ghost' of the second boarder underneath the morphing boarder as the morph takes place and opacity levels are reduced. This is why we want to morph the second boarder from the position of the first, back to his starting position – a bit confusing, but I'm sure you see what I mean.

7. This means it's now time to do the reverse for clip 2. This means that boarder 2 will have 'from' geometries that match the positions of the first boarder, and will warp back to his normal position at the end of the warping sequence.

**8.** This time the process takes seconds rather than hours. You should be able to copy and paste all the masks from the first clip direct to the second. Apply the Re-Flex Warp filter to the second clip and then alter the order of the masks, so instead of pairs of 1 'to', 2 'from', change the layer order so that you have 2 'to' and 1 'from'.

**9.** Now, instead of animating percentage warp from 0 to 100, changing your start and end keyframes from 100 to 0. You don't need to set Opacity keyframes for the second clip. Make sure the second clip is stacked underneath the first (if it isn't already) as you aren't going to see the cross fade with a 100% opaque clip over the top of another!

Well done. That was one of the hardest things I've ever had to explain to anyone. Yes it's tricky, but you have just manually (with a little help from a plug-in!) morphed two moving clips together perfectly. Lucky for you, you have another four pairs worth to do (or use the ones that I have already created – but be warned, without the graft, you aren't improving your skills!).

## Morphed!

Another small point is that you will have to manually add a complete mask on to the edges of the clips to round off the corners. Fortunately for you, I have included the `mask.psd` file, which you can open and directly copy and paste the mask for a perfect fit.

**39.** Now simply (thank goodness!) drag the static_1_end_b.tif file to the timeline, change the anchor point as before to 0 and 0, and then scale over 1 second so the image returns to its position before we started morphing. Make sure you also animate the Tint filter, as before, to make the color in the image revert to grayscale. Don't forget to use Easy Ease.

**40.** As the image is shrinking over the course of the single second, let the next phase commence and have static_2.tif shooting in from the bottom left / left hand side of the screen to the right, and the image scaling up from bottom right towards top left.

**41.** Simply repeat the morphing steps with the next set of clips. Repeat this procedure until you have done all six sets of two clips.

**42.** Now that you have completed all these steps, use some of the static images and animate them moving in straight lines as you see fit, whilst the morphing and boarding is taking place. Be sure not to use any that are from clips that you are currently morphing. Also make sure that these stay grayscaled by using the Tint filter at 100%, so that the action shots stay in color and as the dominant focal point.

At this point, you may find it useful to 'shy' all of the layers we won't be using by clicking the Kilroy (the little guy with his nose poking over a wall; British readers may call him Mr. Chad) circled in the screenshot and then select Shy for each individual layer – giving you a completely freed up timeline.

Our morphing of clips has taken us through to 40 seconds. We need 52 seconds. Fortunately, the final section of the project is one of the easiest and also stays on screen for quite a while – you deserve something easy to do after all those mask manipulations!

**43.** Make sure all moving stills have moved off the screen.

## Text!

Okay, so we had the meat of the sequence sorted, but that didn't entirely solve everything – how were we going to finish the sequence? Clearly, we had to get a logo and the name of the event on the screen at some point, or we weren't getting paid! Now, the design style for the logo, etc had come from another design agency (oh the joys of cross agency projects) and it wasn't a gem. Some bright spark had decided, "Wouldn't it be stunningly original to use the golden stars of the European Union as a logo and then write 'European Snowboarding Championship' underneath it?" We'd already nicely organized something genuinely impressive, and didn't want it ruined by a duff ending, so we asked if we could keep the feel but not write all the words in one straight long line across the screen. Eventually we worked out a compromise that allowed us to do something a little bit more fun.

We decided to use the Stroke commands to spell out the word 'European', which would fill the lion's share of the space, with the 'Snowboarding Championship' text shooting in below. To give the Stroke filter some substance we added Bevel Alpha (edges would have worked just fine) and some Drop Shadow. Despite the dark background, it still gave the text that slightly raised edge. These days, we would be using Maya Paint Effects (which gives more control and better looking strokes), and probably using the 3D layer effects to raise the Logo and text off the screen at a slight angle.

To leave the right kind of impression with the audience, we wanted to be able to keep the fun, atmospheric feel of the initial sequence chunk, rather than finishing with just the stars and the logo – why not make our music work for us? Too often in AE, production people (animators, creative directors – you know who you are and you're all responsible!) find a piece of vaguely suitable sound, maybe spend an hour or two tweaking it in Sound Forge, and then straight in the audio channel. We had already surpassed that rather narrow usage of sound by having our audio waveform animation thumping in the background. However, to take it that one final step, we decided to animate the position, rotation and scale attributes, so that the words in the logo looked like they were being pumped forward by the force of the bassline.

It is actually possible to automate this process by using a little scripting trickery in motion math. However, given the words would only be thumping to the bass for a matter of seconds, it barely seemed worth straining the gray matter, so we took the easy way out and keyframed everything manually. One up for the slackers!

Our version here is a little different, we're X-treme rather than European, although in some cases we may be both.

**44.** Create a new solid, called 'X-treme'. Use the Basic Text filter on this layer, typing in 'X-treme' and using the bulkiest, sans serif font you have. We're using Raphael, but every computer has a different selection of fonts, so choose the one you like best from your collection.

**45.** Now change the color of your text to white and increase the size of the text to about 144 point (2 inches). Turn on the quality switch as well. Apply a Drop Shadow (Effects > Perspective > Drop Shadow) and from the same menu apply the Bevel Alpha effect. Increase the Edge Thickness of the bevel to 4 and the Drop Shadow to 10.

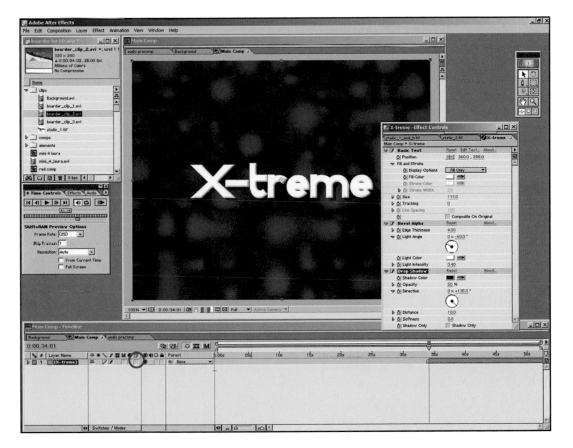

**46.** Now for some new technology. Click the 3D button, circled in the last screenshot. Press R on the layer to access the rotation commands. You will not just have x and y axis to work on now, but x, y and z, so we can alter the way the text is going to dynamically shoot on to the screen. Set x rotation to – 50 and z rotation to +40.

**47.** Position the X-treme text in the center of the screen. Now copy the layer twice. Change the text to 'Snowboarding' and 'Championship' respectively, whilst also changing the font to Arial or Arial MT, depending on your personal preference. Position the text as shown in the screenshot. If you hadn't got Raphael handy to use as a font, you can position the championships layer as you see fit.

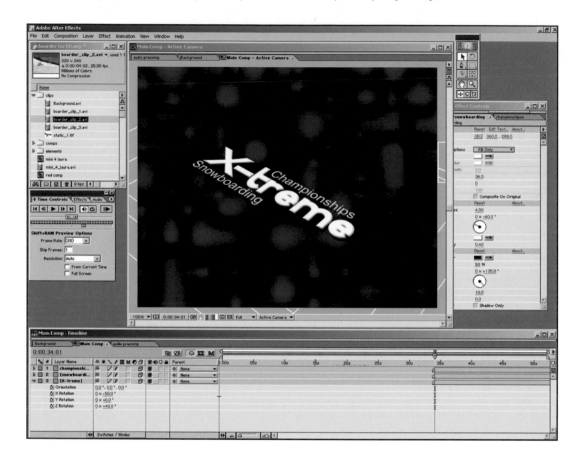

**48.** Set a keyframe at the start of the X-treme layer, and make another keyframe 1 second after the first. Select the first keyframe and drag the layer parallel to the way the text was lying.

**49.** Do the same for the other layers, each with a 1-second stagger, so that the first layer would be the equivalent of entering the screen horizontally and the other words vertically from the top and bottom. If you zoom out, the position of the layers would look like this:

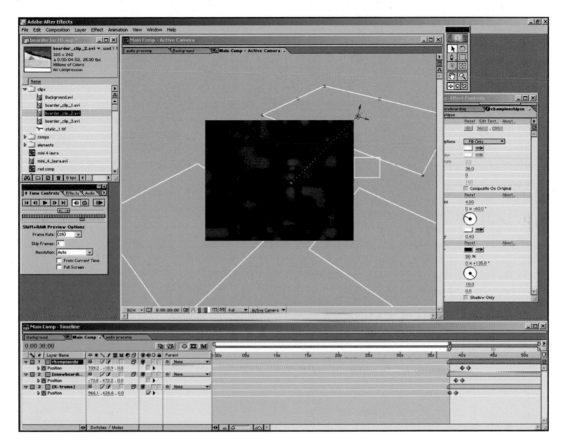

**50.** This time use Easy Ease in to make the animation less linear, with a marked slow down at the end of the movement.

Quite nice, but a little bit flat. Let's use a nice shiny new light – we certainly didn't have such luxury when I first created this clip!

**51.** Create a new light (Layer > New > Light), keeping the default settings. We want to position the light above the text and animate the point of interest (where the spot of the spotlight actually focuses on) so that it sweeps up and down the text. We have made the intensity of the light 140%. The x, y, z position of the light is 377, 110, -190. The x y, z position of the point of interest is 490, 375, 0.

**52.** Animate the point of interest, using the standard Easy Ease on the keyframes to give a natural sweeping effect. I recommend animating the sweeps from 1 to 2 seconds, varying slightly, until the end of the clip. On the last 2 keyframes of the clip, also animate the cone angle from the default 90 degrees, to 180. This will enlarge the cone of the light and allow all of the text to be seen on screen.

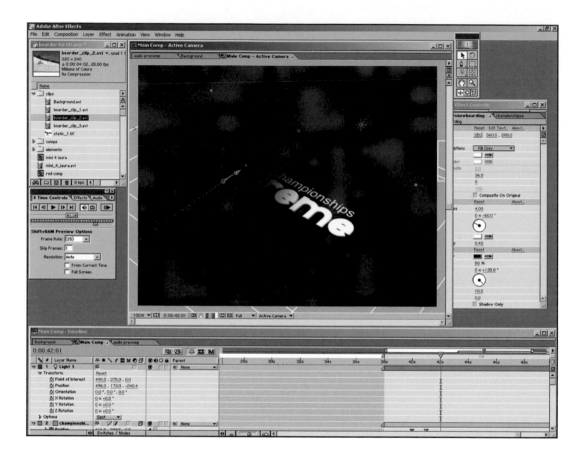

## Putting it all together

After a few final touches, fading the background up from black, fading in the audio and altering a few timings for certain events to happen, everything was in the bag. We transferred the sequence to humble old VHS for an initial approval, and lo and behold, the client was highly satisfied and didn't request any changes. Now that's something you won't find happening every day of the week! One of the benefits of working on a more obscurely scheduled program! We also made sure to alter the keyframe Bezier curves so that everything didn't occur in a linear, mechanical way – although our laziness showed through again as we often opted for good old 'easy ease'.

Nearly there, the finish line is in sight! All we need to do is add and repeat our audio-waveform elements from earlier, and fade up from black at the start.

**53.** Un-shy all the layers, unhide the two audio waveforms we created, and hide all other elements for now, as it will take ages to keyframe and render otherwise. Also set the Quality tab to low quality and the resolution to half. Now, every 5 seconds animated both the audio waveform's start and end points so they move up and down, but never quite in alignment. Set Opacity to 0 and keyframe at 8 seconds to 100%. Keyframe the opacity of the background to 0% at 0 seconds and 100% at 2 seconds.

**54.** Un-hide the rest of the layers, and there you go – a few changes from the original (damn those lawyers), but pretty damn impressive all the same!

## That's it

We've done it, used After Effects to create an fun, eye-catching and interesting television trailer, and all without losing too much hair. Check out the finished version on the CD.

Here we've been creative within some quite harsh boundaries of time and brief, later in the book I've another project to show you where we've been able to do pretty much what we want. But first these messages...

# SIMON TYSZKO

Simon Tyszko is a fine artist, filmmaker, and photographer. You can see some of his work at www.theculture.net.

Simon works mostly as a gallery-based artist, in a diverse range of media, including neon, video, film, books, glass, fabrics and assembled objects.

He has won a number of awards for various works including two categories in the London Photographic awards 1998. Sponsored by tomato, he won a Creative Review Creative Futures award for his work with sound in November 1997.

Simon often produces commercial work in association with a number of other artists, under the umbrella of theculture, a loose-knit collection of artists, designers, architects and musicians, whose work frequently defies traditional boundaries.

theculture are at various times, and not exclusively: Simon Tyszko, Gina Birch, Anand Zenz, Olimax, Oliver Knights and Nao Shimizu.

Recent projects from theculture have included music videos for New Order, Beth Orton and rough trade records. Web sites have included an award-winning site for Primal Scream (www.primalscream.org) and the development of online artificial intelligence (www.olimax.com), where you can see the work of the Soho-based new media company created by Olimax specifically for advanced multimedia projects.

Gina Birch and Simon Tyszko are currently working on her new solo album for rock star records as a follow up to her work as founder member of The Raincoats (Rough Trade and Geffen records).

Simon's film has included the experimental digital work Karamii (featured in this chapter) and an award-winning short made entirely from miniature cameras hidden in a pair of shoes and presented in synchronized split screen. Oliver Knights (co-director of Karamii) has gone on to international music fame with his Mercury Music Prize and Brit Award nominated band Turin Brakes.

theculture are increasingly engaged in agitation/propaganda work, most notably in the recent placement of a suicide bomber Barbie doll (www.theculture.net/barbie) in London's Institute of Contemporary Arts, which is presently at the centre of a media storm throughout Europe, including wildly conflicting reviews in most of the high-end press (see www.guardian.co.uk/weekend/story/0,3605,774949,00.html and www.observer.co.uk/review/story/0,6903,768757,00.html).

It is this ability to make people sit up and think that marks the unique diversity of theculture. Hopefully they will continue going where no one has gone before.

'fries'
portrait,
manipulated image 1996

'buy nothing'
car, smoke , neon 1997

# VIDEO ART, LET'S DANCE
## Split-screen FX and Video Choreography

Karamii is an experimental video work made to explore the growing possibilities within After Effects and also as a stylish way to collage elements from several other video projects.

At theculture our work is conceived mostly as fine art gallery productions, yet this boundary often crosses over to the commercial world, drawing from and contributing back, from advertising to music videos and interactive media including web sites for Primal Scream (the band) and various record company and fashion projects.

Started as a small scale project on an old, beige G3 Apple Mac, Karamii grew into a little monster, ending up with over 150 layers of video, straining every last byte from the small processor and eventually appearing as a full screen short film in a West End cinema release.

In reality, we cannot recommend you do this alone at home without the presence of a trained physician, yet despite the risks, in the end it was worth it.

There is an article about Karamii at the Adobe web site, www.adobe.co.uk/motion/features/karamii.

We started the project by gathering various elements together and processing them for look and feel. We then rendered them off and added them to the final composition. We also shot a number of new sequences, which would act as the stylistic glue holding the work together.

Many of the techniques we simply made up as we went along, finding many treats and surprises along the way. But, most importantly, we played extensively with the multitude of tools available in After Effects, remaining open to the exciting and the new.

It really was a process of discovery, and here I will describe some of the key elements we used in the production and hope you can take these as a starting point for your own journey. Since we completed Karamii we have used many of the techniques in a wide range of productions, including most recently promos for both Beth Orton and New Order.

## Choreography

From the beginning we wanted to work with split screen, taking inspiration from classic 1960's heist type films such as The Thomas Crown Affair, which would give us a strong visual identity and also allow us to take full advantage of the layering, animation, compositing and visual effects possibilities in After Effects.

Once we've decided to work with multiple images on screen, we had to find pleasing proportions, aspects and ratios using the screen as a canvas on which to compose with multiple moving images. We didn't want to recreate something that had already been done; this had to be new and fresh.

Once we started to place the various elements together on screen and started moving them about, we realized that there was amazing potential in considering the various clips not only as video but also as graphical elements. This soon developed into a form of video choreography as we settled into conventions which allowed us to move the individual elements gracefully on and off the screen, forming an aesthetic and balanced relationship to the overall composition. From this practical consideration grew one of the central features of the whole production. We soon developed a system whereby the individual screens/clips were reduced to either horizontal or vertical bars and then swept into the composition.

We then abstracted this further, working with loops of filmed static and colored bars, overlaying and working with the more narrative video clips. As this progressed, our early test renders fitted gloriously with the soundtrack we had made earlier (using Steinberg Cubase) and it was now just a matter of pushing through from frame 1 and putting the whole project together.

To really start off with a practical understanding of the processes involved in the making of Karamii, I thought it would be useful to outline a simple project that only requires the After Effects application, with no external video, yet introduces a number of the tools and techniques we used intensively later in the project. In reality, this was the last thing we did as it became a culture splash at the end of the cinema release, yet here we shall start off with this simple and hopefully pleasing animation.

## Flying text

For the end titles we created an effect whereby the word 'theculture' was broken up into individual letters, which spun in from space to form the title. The letters were blurred and aged to form the final composition. It's a simple enough idea, but very effective.

1. Open up a new project and create a composition to whatever size you feel will suit your project. Create a solid layer (CONTROL/CMD + Y) the same size as the composition, on which we will create the completed text to use as a template for the animated layers.

**Solid Settings**

Name: Solid 1

Size

Width: 720    100.0%
                        of composition size
Height: 576    100.0%

Units: pixels

☐ Lock Aspect Ratio to 5:4

Make Comp Size

Color

Cancel    OK

**2.** Next, using the basic text effect bundled with After Effects, we will create a template layer containing the text as you wish it to appear, aligning the text using the Center option.

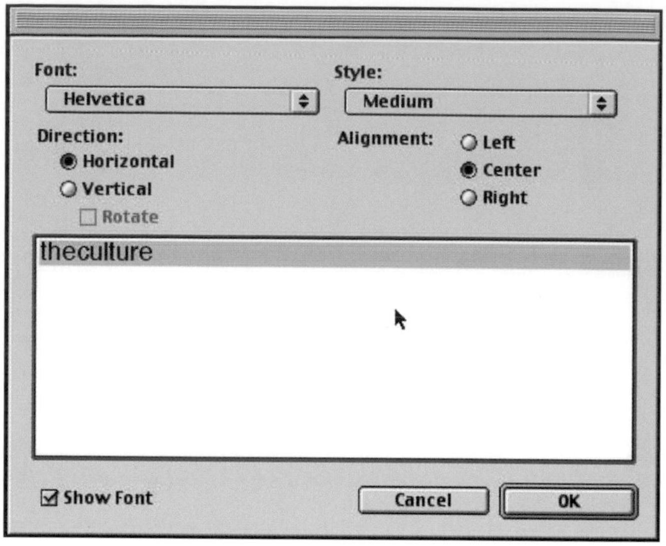

**Font:** Helvetica

**Style:** Medium

**Direction:**
● Horizontal
○ Vertical
☐ Rotate

**Alignment:**
○ Left
● Center
○ Right

theculture

☑ Show Font    Cancel    OK

**3.** Using the controls in the Effect Controls window you can set the text size, and choose between combinations of fill, stroke, and letter spacing (using the Tracking control).

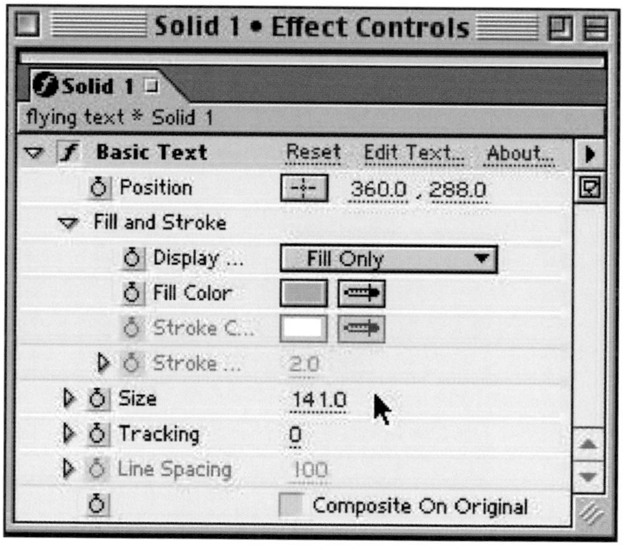

**Solid 1 • Effect Controls**

Solid 1

flying text * Solid 1

▽ *f* **Basic Text**    Reset    Edit Text...    About...

○ Position    360.0 , 288.0

▽ Fill and Stroke

○ Display ...    Fill Only

○ Fill Color

○ Stroke C...

▷ ○ Stroke ...    2.0

▷ ○ Size    141.0

▷ ○ Tracking    0

▷ ○ Line Spacing    100

○    Composite On Original

This is how the text will be laid out finally, and we can therefore use this layer to place the individual letters. Like much of After Effects this is quite painstaking – meticulous yet ultimately rewarding. We first need to separate the letters.

**4.** Initially duplicate the template layer by highlighting it in the timeline and selecting Duplicate from the Edit menu (or CONTROL/CMD + D).

**5.** Then, making sure that you have the duplicate selected, open the effect controls for that layer (CONTROL/CMD + SHIFT + T) and select the Edit Text option. Once in this menu delete all the letters apart from the first 't'.

This leaves us with two layers on the timeline – the first (our template) reading 'theculture' and the second reading 't', which is now in the middle of the composition.

6.  We are now going to move the 't' so that it's directly above the corresponding letter on the template, using the horizontal position handle. If necessary we can tweak it using the arrow keys.

7.  Once we have completed this layer we will repeat this procedure for each individual letter/layer. For good housekeeping I would suggest renaming each layer as you duplicate it. The steps are:

1.  Duplicate (CONTROL/CMD + D)

2.  Rename (RETURN)

3.  Open effect controls (CONTROL/CMD + SHIFT + T)

4. Edit text

5. Change letter

6. Re-position

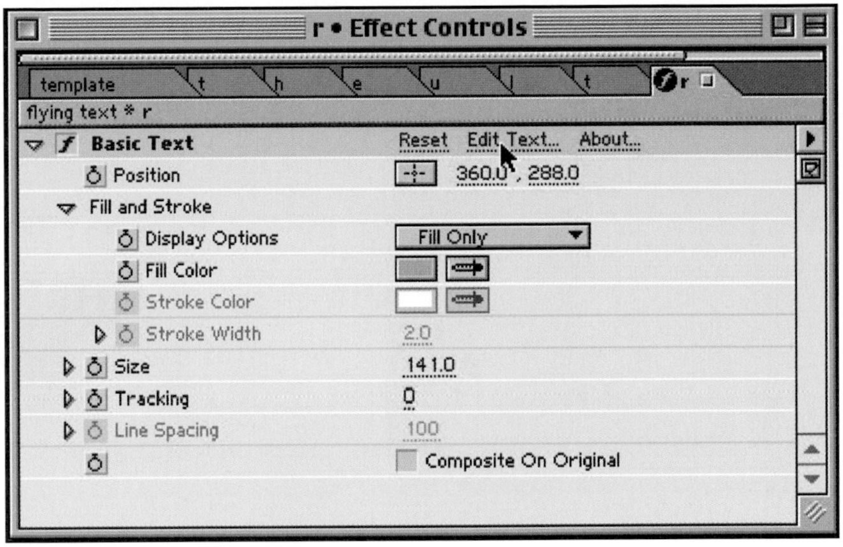

It's good to note here that letters like the 'e', which are repeated in the text, can be duplicated a number of times and After Effects denotes this with an asterix * added to the name.

8. When all the individual letters have been created we can turn off the visibility of the template layer, leaving the layers above perfectly recreating the text we wish to end up with.

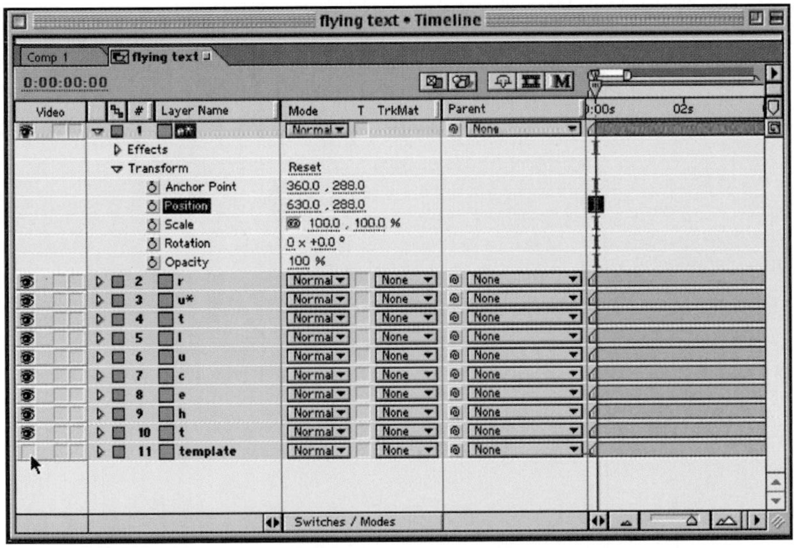

So now we are ready to play with the various controls to animate the sequence. For this effect I'm going to need the basic 3D effect added to each layer, so here it's easiest to select multiple layers on the timeline and then add the effect to them all.

**9.** Just select all on the timeline, and then deselect the template layer by SHIFT-clicking the template layer.

**10.** So now with all desired layers selected go to Effects > Perspective > Basic 3D.

**11.** Next we should decide how long we want the action to last. Here I'm choosing about 5 seconds.

**12.** Next we must create a series of keyframes on each layer for every parameter we are going to change. These should be at the start of the timeline and at the 5-second point on the timeline. To do this we open up each layer using the layer arrow on the timeline and then tick the clock beside each parameter we are going to use. In this case it will be Basic 3D, Swivel, Tilt, Distance to Image, Transform, Position, Scale, and Rotation.

There's no harm in adding keyframes now for any other parameters that you might wish to experiment with later, as it's easier to add them and not use them than to go back and add them later.

13. Next we need to copy all these keyframes to the 5-second mark. Using the SHIFT key, click on each of the keyframes you wish to use (or select them by click-dragging with the mouse) and copy them using (CONTROL/CMD + C).

14. Then simply move the time marker to the appropriate place on the timeline (5 seconds) and paste them into place (CONTROL/CMD + V). This gives us an identical set of keyframes at the start and end points for the animation in this layer.

The copying and pasting of keyframes is an immensely timesaving and useful feature of After Effects and can be used in many different circumstances. It's really worth taking the time to experiment with this facility. Throughout our projects we often copy complex animations and effect sequences and adapt them for new layers. We shall be using much more of this for animating other layers. This technique is a fantastic timesaver and good housekeeping.

**15.** Repeat the pasting for each letter/layer, at the end of which we should have a series of start and end keyframes for each letter/layer.

So, now that we have our start and end points it's time to create the animation. The end points have the text assembled as we want it to read, so that no matter what we do in the proceeding frames, we know that the text will end up reading as we wish. Therefore, at this point, it's possible to play and experiment with all the parameters we have entered, and any others you can think of adding. As long as the end frames are set to what we want to see it's difficult to go wrong.

**16.** To create the specific title sequence used in Karamii, we shall first return to the beginning and delete (select layer and delete) the template layer. This isn't strictly necessary, but good housekeeping is essential in After Effects as things can soon get out of hand.

Now we have one layer for each letter, that's 10, and the composition looks like this:

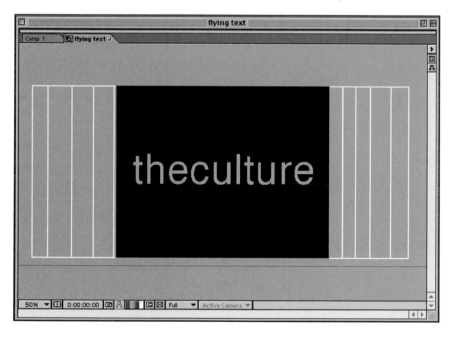

**17.** Make sure the time marker is set right at the start of the composition.

Clicking the arrows either side of the keyframe indicator will take you either back to the last or forward to the next keyframe. It's a great timesaver when navigating through complex compositions.

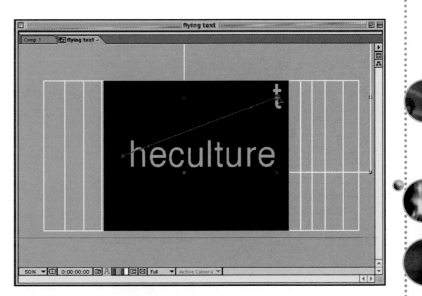

## It's alive

We'll now deal with the position of the letters.

**18.** To start the animation, make sure you are at the start and select the first letter 't' from the timeline. Then in the work area move the 't' layer to where you want it to appear (usually slightly off screen).

We can check the animations for speed and look during production as frequently as we'd like by simply trying either a Ram Preview to see the actual letter animate, or a Wireframe Preview to judge the speed of the layer.

So that you can see as much as possible, set the resolution of the main window to as low as necessary. It's an equation of the amount of RAM available/resolution/time you can preview. As ever the more RAM the better.

In the instance of our project, setting the resolution to a quarter will allow us to view the whole 5 seconds, and is more than adequate to see clearly how the animation is working. However, when previewing more complex effects that are image critical, a higher resolution and shorter time should be used.

**19.** So a Ram Preview here (Composition > Preview > Ram Preview) will show the 't' floating back to place.

## Around and around she goes...

So far, so simple. Next we can try rotation.

**20.** Once again, at the first keyframes set the rotation slider under the Transform menu to 1 degree (of rotation).

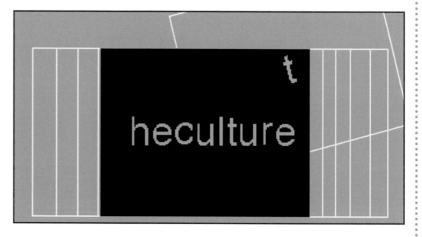

**21.** Try the Ram Preview again. The 't' now spins as it returns.

**22.** Try something similar with the Basic 3D. Set the Swivel to 1 degree and the Distance to Image at around 40.

As we preview this we can see it's really starting to get a really stylish motion going. By trying variations with each of the other layers we can quickly have a great title splash. Try negative as well as positive values, play a little, go a little too far, then go back and show a little restraint (you'll find this particularly difficult, well I do anyway).

Here we can see all the various motion paths we have created:

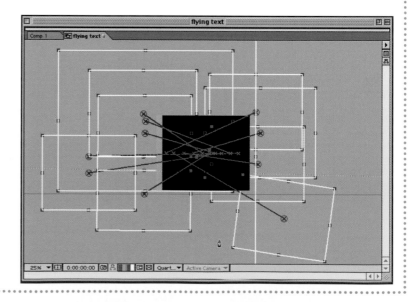

It's a simple matter to add keyframes at any point in the animation, to allow you to add direction changes and curves into the path.

23. Simply by dragging the letter around in the work area, we create a new position/keyframe. Initially this will give a jagged motion to the letter's movement. For this animation though, we want the motion to be smooth, so here we should use the Bezier curve controls to smooth things out a little and give us another level of finesse.

24. Place the time control to somewhere in the middle of the animation and move the letter, creating a new keyframe in the process.

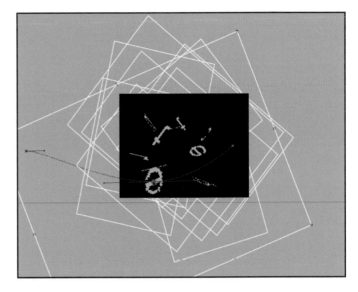

Notice the Bezier handles appearing either side of the pointer. Operating these will create the smoothest changes in path, speed and direction.

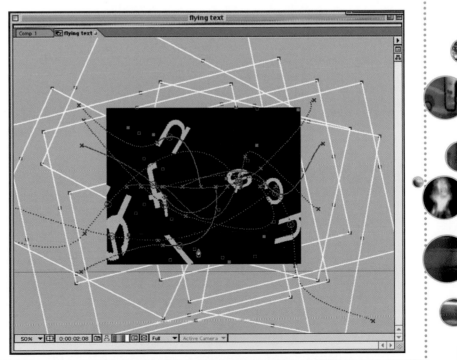

## You've got the look

Having created a smooth and satisfying animation we will now give it a better overall look.

**25.** First we are going to add an adjustment layer above all the others in the timeline.

Adjustment layers are extremely useful for adding effects to multiple layers. They affect all layers below them in the timeline. You can add a new one at Layer > New > Adjustment Layer.

**26.** With the adjustment layer selected we then added a Gaussian Blur

This filter is a firm favorite for softening and smoothing out text in video work, leaving us with a smoky and smooth appearance for our flying text sequence. It's especially useful when your compression codec is one that tends to make text blocky.

## Collecting the elements

The flying text composition is just one tiny aspect of our project; there are plenty of other elements, from a wide variety of sources. Although working with the most up to date digital processes, we wanted the piece to have a strong 'analog' feel, like listening to CDs on a valve amplifier.

## Static & Super 8

We gathered some of our elements by videoing directly from the TV or computer screen, which is probably just a stylistic quirk, but fun nonetheless. Here we took a section of static from a de-tuned television.

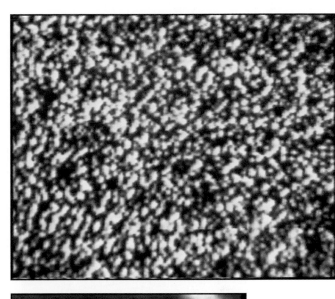

And here we had a selection of old Super 8 film reels from the early 1960's. These were expertly and carefully transferred to digital media by the simple expedient of projecting them onto a white wall and videoing from there.

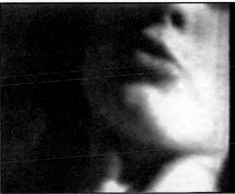

Some of the older video clips we used from much older video work was produced using a much more extreme version of this, like this 1995 gallery projection Sublime Burn.

The original was shot using a Hi 8 camera, with the only light source being the match in my hand.

To further distress the image it was transferred onto VHS (a disgustingly lossy format) and then played back on a TV monitor and re-shot onto Hi 8, maybe once or twice, I really can't quite remember. The result is an extremely moody and primitive feeling video clip with a unique analog kind of aura. For Karamii we updated the piece in After Effects, by adding the PS+Lens Flare effect, using motion tracking and the Wiggler.

Sometimes it's still a good thing to try things outside of the computer, as this will often provide off-the-wall results.

## Keying text video

As well as the choreographic manipulation of video clips, much of Karamii made good use of various keying effects to drop out selected sections on various layers. This was especially true of the text layers, which cut through the whole piece. In this example we shall look at the preparation of the text layers and the keying used to drop out the backgrounds.

The text was created in Macromedia Director as a random generator using 800 iconic words and phrases. When played straight and filmed in a lock off it was actually quite dull, so we switched to a hand-held camera view and panned in and out of the screen, not being afraid to crop, lose focus or miss the words as they flew over the screen.

The result was a truly dynamic selection of text clips, which we knew we would wish to use extensively. In this example we will have a simple two-layer section, with the black background text over a saturated color clip of some flowers.

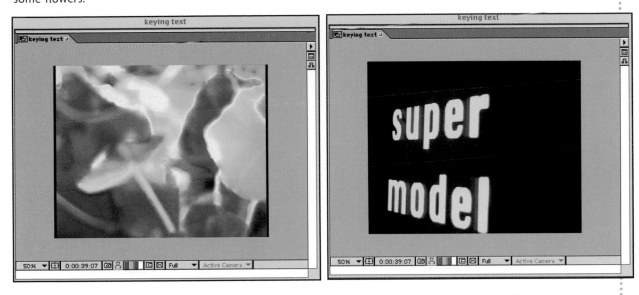

It's important to bear in mind that when using keys, the quality of the source material is more important than ever. Even the compression codecs used in modern DV footage are considered to be too full of artifacts for professional keying. As a result, we decided to work with the limitations rather than being put off by them, but anything less than DV quality can become really problematic.

**1.** With the text in the layer above the flower, go to the Effects menu and select Keying > Color Key.

This key is most useful when dropping out a solid color background such as the traditional chromakey blue, but with the flexibility of After Effects any color can be chosen as long as the image to remain is free of that hue.

In this example, it's a relatively straightforward black background, yet as it was shot directly from a computer screen the blacks are never really black, and the shadows and focus blurs will provide some surprises.

2.  To start off, select the Dropper tool from the Effect Controls window, and place it over the area to be keyed out (in this case the black).

This will remove most of the black background, but still leave visible areas not quite matching the dropper selection.

To remove this we experiment with the various options available in the Effect Controls window for the Color Key effect.

**3.** Color Tolerance is the most important here. Gradually sliding it up will remove colors closely related to the selection, until eventually it will start to remove the text we actually want to keep, so we find the most pleasing balance.

**4.** Next we experiment with Edge Thin to take the key back into the text. A negative figure will bring back the background around the text, rather like a stroke effect.

**5.** The Edge Feather control adds a pleasing softness to the text, with a gentle amount of the background fading around the text.

Experimenting with various degrees of all these controls can give quite fantastic and surprising results. Go on, play!

Next we experimented with the layer modes. Here the background becomes visible through the text as variable and produces interesting color changes as the background changes.

**6.** This time we settled on Difference.

Along with the Color Key you can use any combination of effects from the Key menu, and other tools, such as, Simple Choker, Matte Choker, Alpha Levels, and Spill Suppressor, which are all available in the Production Bundle. All these will have different and varying results, depending on the source footage being keyed.

As each video clip you wish to key out will be very different, experimentation will bring many unexpected and pleasing effects. This is most defiantly an art and not a science.

## It's not the getting there, it's the journey

Another major section of the work is the journey through the city. This segment was created especially for Karamii and acts as a strong and recurrent thematic device.

For the journey we were looking to give a strong impression of speed, and a high degree of dislocation from everyday reality. So, after trying various camera/film combinations, we settled on the Sony VX1000, using a slow shutter speed, for a blurred image and a strong, saturated color effect.

Most of this was completed in one take, with Oli Knights holding the camera whilst hanging out of the sunroof of my car.

7.  This kind of footage looks like a series of blurred still images when played back at normal speed, so to give the dynamic we were after we speeded the footage up using the Time Stretch (Layer > Time Stretch) in After Effects, and then rendered it out and re-imported it for use in the composition.

8.  We experimented with various time adjustments and settled on speeding up the clip three times. This made the journey appear almost at normal speed (which was originally quite fast), but it was now blurred, smoothed and highly stylized.

9.  At the same as speeding up the video, we also tripled the speed of the audio track. Although it would have been simple to separate them off, the now frantic sound of the wind screaming through the mike added an unexpected drama to the visuals, so this was added to the final mix.

10. To further accentuate the look, we added a little extra color saturation from the Adjust menu, taking it up a notch with a value of 26%.

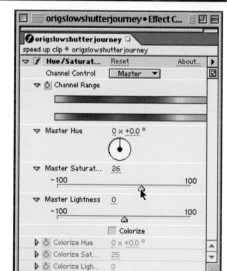

If you experiment with the saturation controls, you will find that there comes a point when the color becomes too saturated and the image starts to break up and pixilate.

**Before**

**After**

**11.** With the speed and look now exact, it's just a simple procedure to export the work area as a QuickTime movie set to DV PAL best settings, and then re-import into the project.

# Preparing for video choreography

Having gathered together a wide range of clips, we set about putting the final composition together. With such a variety of footage there were bound to be some problems, but eventually we solved them all, and here are a few pointers.

## Field goals

As we were going to be scaling and moving clips over and above each other with various degrees of transparency, and using different layer modes, it was extremely important for the clips' fields to be interpreted correctly when importing. There is much written about this in the After Effects help files and on various sites, and I highly recommend you read up on this. I shall only be able to give a brief outline here.

Broadcast video is made up of two images or fields, which are interlaced to provide the image you see broadcast onto your screen. This is a convention dating back to the earliest days of video and television, yet still has relevance today.

PAL and NTSC footage can be different in whether the lower field or upper field is presented first. Getting your fields mixed up or in the wrong order can look terrible, especially where the scale or proportions are to be changed.

In the production of Karamii we learned this the hard way, with perfectly good looking clips suddenly appearing jagged and distorted when we started moving them around. Take a look at these example images:

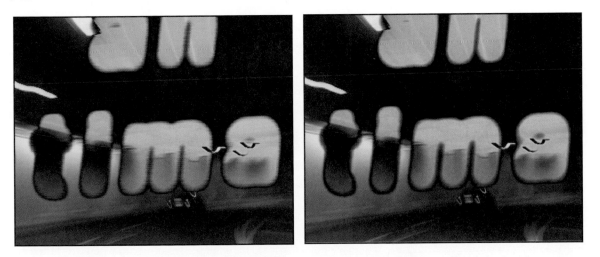

In the first picture you can clearly see the jagged lines around the text layer when the Separate Fields option is off, and in the second you can see the much smoother and correct look when the Separate Fields option is correctly set to lower field first.

As bad as it can look and as complex as it sounds, it's relatively easy to sort out upper from lower. For a start, After Effects can do this automatically for you when you import the original footage. This is done using the `interpretation rules.txt` document in the After Effects folder. This document contains a series of rules for After Effects to follow when importing footage, and the document can be edited to suit your needs.

I have often found versions of After Effects which don't contain the correct localized versions of this file. I have included the rules for importing DV PAL footage for you here:

```
# assume PAL DV is D1 aspect, lower-field
720, 576, 25, "MooV", "dvcp" = 768/720, L, *, *
```

Simply copy this into `interpretation rules.txt` in your After Effects folder and it will interpret the footage for you.

Even without this, it's a simple matter to change or check once footage has been already been imported.

It's also good to note that this is the same dialog box that you can set a clip to loop in. For instance, our clip of the TV static was very short, so we looped it about 20 times.

## Masks

Imported video clips will often not have the image going right to the edge of the frame, so when we started to have the clips expand, contract and move, these black edges were initially a real problem.

Notice the black lines at the sides of the clip. These are not normally a problem, as they exist well outside of the action area.

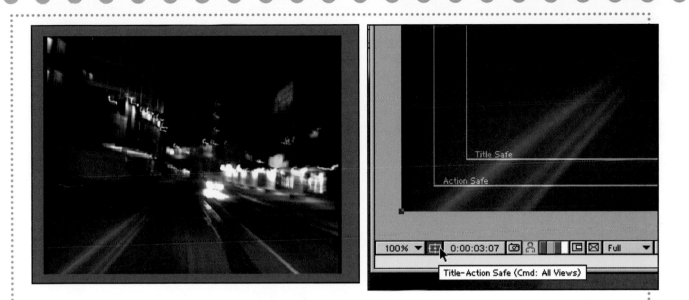

We decided to create masks for each layer and, rather than have hard edges to the shapes we were creating, we decided to apply a strong feather to them, leaving them soft and in keeping with the smooth feel of the overall project.

1. Select the Rectangle Mask tool, and then drag the tool across the project window to create a new mask.

In this illustration I have made the composition window gray to make it clearer. Masks can also be easily created by double-clicking the layer in the timeline and opening the layer window. The mask can be drawn here and the results can be immediately seen in the main work area.

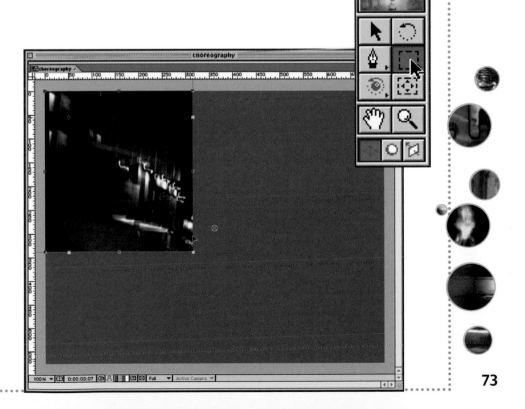

2. A real time saver here is to make the first mask and then copy and paste it to other layers, simply by highlighting the mask, copying it, highlighting the layer you want it to be on, and pasting. The feather settings can be added later or pasted at the same time.

3. We wanted quite a broad feather so we masked off around 60 pixels all round the clip.

4. On the timeline we opened the mask's controls and set the Mask Feather to about 57 pixels. With the background set back to black you can see the results.

5. Returning to the timeline we opened the Transform panel and, in the Scale, de-selected the ratio lock so we could adjust the horizontal and vertical separately.

And now we're ready to start choreographing/animating our work.

## Dance

All the elements are prepared and in place. Here I shall explain a short section, illustrating how I go about making things move in a cohesive and intelligible way.

If you look back to the flying text section you can see how adding keyframes is the basis of animating in After Effects. The very same principles apply for the larger video sections as applied to the simple text piece. This section of the chapter steps through the production of a short section of Karamii using 5 clips, and the keying animation techniques we used in the making of the flying text clips.

We will also be using one of the text clips that we prepared and applied the keying filters to when we were preparing the project.

This is what we're after: the final look of this section with the text floating above, a band of static flying back and forth, two slow shutter speeded up city clips, and finally a solid layer which is set to classic transfer mode and has a customized film damage filter (named when saved as St Trinians) applied to give it that totally dirty and analog grunged up look.

For the building and assembling of a section like this, production time can be speeded up by turning off unnecessary effects until you specifically need them. For instance, every time I move anything the CineLook Film Damage (www.digieffects.com) effect takes forever to re-draw, making meaningful production impossible. So I toggle this effect on and off, only setting it on when I need to check a crucial frame look.

**1.** Having got this composition pretty much as I want it to look, I will create keyframes for every parameter at the start and end of the work area, pretty much as we did in the flying text section.

**2.** Then we go back to the beginning (the first keyframe) and take most of the elements off the screen and change their proportion, using the Transform handles on the timeline. This creates a simple motion path and animation for each layer as we do so.

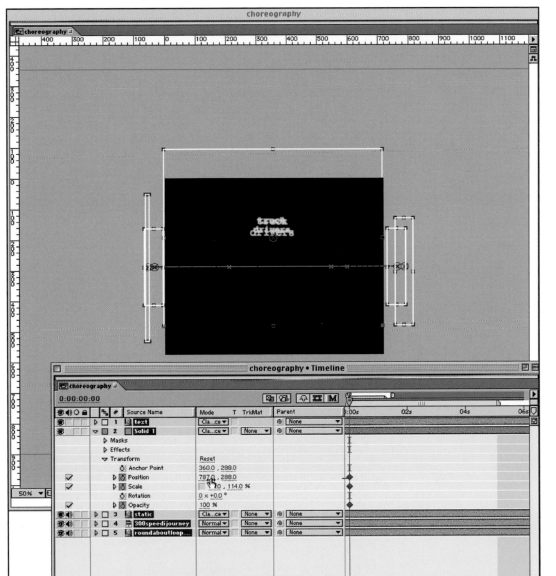

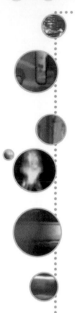

Here you can see the animation halfway through a 5-second movement. To test the speed of the layer's movement, it's quite a good idea to try a number of Wireframe Previews, making sure you have all the layers selected.

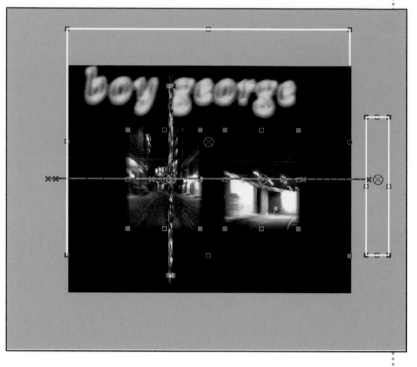

3. Simply by adjusting the end keyframes you can change the speed of the animation, and the rate at which any of the parameters vary.

4. Bearing this in mind and using the copy/paste (as we had with our flying text), it's possible to re-use a complex series of movements and effects on a new layer.

By experimenting with the Keyframe Assistant, motion math, the Wiggler and the Smoother, it's possible to radically alter a series of keyframes, creating something quite new.

Already we have a fantastic looking section of video going here. Through a combination of well-selected clips, interesting colorization, a stylish use of movement, and a relatively gentle use of effects, it's possible to make something really startling happen.

5. Once everything is in place it's just a matter of spending the time to put together all the elements and sections to make the overall composition work.

One of the most exciting techniques we found in this experimentation was the addition of effects to masked adjustment layers, and then flying them over and around the composition. This came directly from following one process into another. Experimentation.

As ever, I can't stress enough how important it is to play with this program as a practical process of discovery. The GUI (graphical user interface) on our computers has developed as an intuitive device, and therefore I personally find it easier to steam into a project allowing myself the luxury of mistakes and the huge rewards of discovery. Working like this I can use the inbuilt help files to enable me to work out solutions to problems I encounter in my own process, rather than using them as guides as to what's possible.

On a practical level, Karamii became quite unwieldy and required many sections to be rendered out and then re-imported or edited together, using either Premiere or, more recently, Final Cut Pro.

Through a process of trial and error we created an immensely satisfying piece of work, and when we first digitally projected the piece onto a full sized cinema screen (in the Metro cinema in London's Soho), we were literally speechless.

Experiment, play, create.

## Special thanks

Olimax: multimedia artist and designer. www.olimax.com

Anand Zenz: artist, designer, architect. www.zenz.net

Gina Birch: filmmaker, musician and fronts the famous band The Raincoats (one of Kurt Cobain's favorites) who are on Kill Rock Star Records.

Oliver Knights: filmmaker and lately has signed a major recording deal with Virgin label Source Records as half of acoustic duo, Turin Brakes. www.turinbrakes.com.

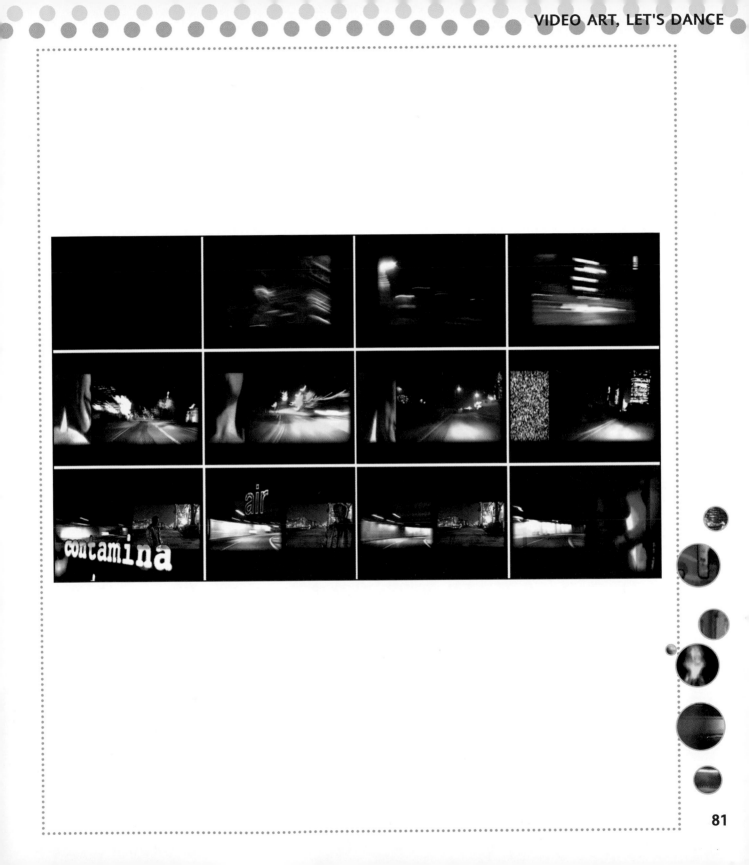

# CHRIS JAMES HEWITT

I was born in Plymouth, UK and raised in Manchester, I found my love for creativity at the early age of 14 when I started to experiment with the likes of Photoshop. After being speed through a four year new media design diploma at Oldham Technical college I was recruited by top northern based design agency Computer Love. After spending just over a year and a half at Computer Love I had worked on projects such as DrMartens.com and had been taught the basics in motion graphics.

I stated my own personal web site Dstrukt.net two years ago and have since produced work for the likes of Computer Arts, Digital vision and BD4D. I has also been involved with many online projects including work for Pixel surgeon, Design For Freedom, BD4D and many more. Currently, I live in London where I work as graphic/ motion designer for WAX New Media.

Moving to London not only changed myself as a person, but my work and what it stands for. Within the first few days of living here I was getting crazy surges of inspiration and idea after idea for new moving image concepts. I think that not only do your natural surroundings help creativity, but also the people you interact with day in day out.

Meeting up with friends, seeing new places and hearing unfamiliar sounds all adds to my inspiration. There's just so much going on and it's hard not to absorb it.

When I was younger and still to this day I had a huge fascination with the ocean. The way it shifts form and moves in such an elegant but yet also aggressive way always puts me in awe. The majority of my work doesn't reflect my love for the sea but I find having something so natural and raw that you visually admire can really help and keep you from hitting those major design blocks.

Aside from motion design, and my second passion for 3D art forms, I love photography. Just recently I came across a Finnish photographer who'd captured some amazing imagery of people submerged underwater. Using intense lighting the final outcome of his work was amazing, the variation in color and form was mind blowing. I found myself taking note of the colors and the way the lighting bled through the water. I wanted to integrate these natural elements into my work.

Producing beautiful artwork is one thing, but producing beautiful artwork that holds substance and imagination is another. Hopefully I can take Dstrukt further this way.

4

**EAT STATIC**
Relokation Ne™- Abstract animation,
Sound sync and TV FX

Relokation Ne was produced for Event 7 of BD4D London. By Designers for Designers (www.bd4d.com) was set up to bring great new media designers together, at live events around the globe. Its events, which have been hosted in London, Manchester, Paris, Sydney, Los Angeles, New York City and Toronto, enable designers to show their work and network with other designers. The Relokation movie was presented alongside Joost Korngold of Renascent (www.renascent.nl). Joost and myself also presented our motion work at Event 3 of BD4D and were invited back recently to showcase our latest moving image projects.

The movie is an abstract interpretation of my move to London from Manchester at the beginning of 2002. I left Manchester to follow my dream of working in 'the big city' – since I started in the design industry working in London was my main goal. When the opportunity arrived I had to take it with both hands. Also, after spending the majority of my life in Manchester I wanted to try something new and have the chance to meet new people.

The piece represents the ups and downs in life and tries to convey the feeling of growth and development as a person. The last two years for 'me' as a designer and as person have been something I will never forget. I wanted to try and put all my feelings and memories onto screen in a reformed and diluted way. The key was to not give away too much. Even though Relokation is based on my story and my past it can relate to everyone.

To make this work I had to be very careful with what was represented on the screen.

## Preparation, detail

With my main concept for the movie set in place I had to determine smaller elements for the piece, such as colors, typography and sound. These smaller elements can bring your movie to life, and the more consideration you take the better the overall output will be.

The color system sets the mood and overall style of the piece. I chose orange (my particular orange being R=187, G=109, B=61) due to it being a very vibrant and warming color. Orange also contrasts well with the white used for the focal points.

To add more feeling of depth to the movie, I opted for the use of a slight gradient for the background. A darker tone of the original orange was placed at the bottom of the composition, giving the slight impression of perspective.

As Relokation was produced as a movie for the Web, detailing had to be very precise. I had to make sure that all the elements are correctly sized and positioned. I wanted my type to be clear and upfront. I needed a font that was easy to read and at the same time complemented my movie design. Helvetica Neu was the font I chose – not the most original use of typography but simplistic and easy to read. I used a variation of weights from 55 to 75.

Visually, Relokation only tells half the story. The soundtrack was produced by Diagram of Suburban Chaos (www.diagram-of-suburban-chaos.com). The track Mental Wound, is a very emotional track and is paced in such a way that it connected with my overall concept perfectly.

## Let's get to it

On the CD accompanying this book is the AE project file `Relokation.aep`. There are two ways for you to follow the steps here – you can either open the file now and see exactly how I've put my version together, or start a project of your own and make your decisions as you go.

Opening the project file without having the plug-ins that it uses (or demos) installed will bring up an error message, although it will still allow you to investigate the structure of the project. The DE Video Malfunction plug-in demo can be downloaded from www.digieffects.com, and more information about the other plug-ins used is at www.iced.com/ICEeffects_FEC.asp.

1. I gave my movie a Square Pixels canvas of 550x295 and fps of 25. Note that Relokation Ne is a PAL format movie. As the piece was produced for the Web, giving the composition a PAL resolution of 768 x 576 would be too big to be played through a browser. My initial composition was to be 2 minutes in length, and this would be my master After Effects file.

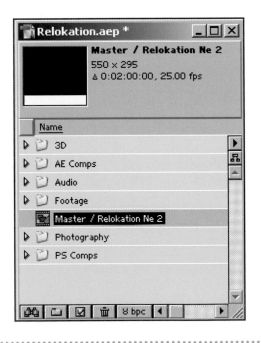

From here I prepared all my composition folders and imported all the elements I needed into AE. As After Effects comps can get very messy and cluttered, I always arrange sub folders in the project window. This way I can keep track of where everything is. My folder list includes: 3D, AE Comps, Audio, Footage, Photography and PS Comps.

This isn't a necessary method but can come in very useful for large scale After Effects work.

Now the main composition is set up we can begin in earnest.

2.  Before I began to animate the introduction for Relokation, the first thing I did was place the soundtrack into the timeline and check the waveform of the track.

The waveform shows you where the beat and the pitch of the audio changes, making it easy for you to manually sync up your animation to the music. Having a moving image piece that is animated well but doesn't flow correctly to music loses half the impact.

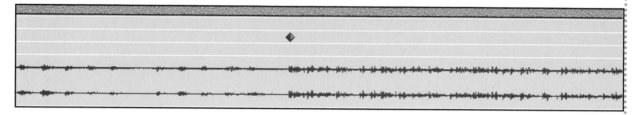

3.  Once the audio is in place we can begin to animate the first sequence. The start of Relokation is a straightforward background fade, from black to the backing gradient of orange.

4.  Once my transparency transition has finished, the title and subtitle text is tweened on using the Gaussian Blur filter (Effect > Blur & Sharpen > Gaussian Blur).

My first keyframe is set at 15 and blends straight through to 0. Whilst this is happening there is also a slight transparency transition occurring at the start.This softens and makes the sequence much easier on the eye. When setting up both transitions, I listened repeatedly to the soundtrack for areas within which the transition would fit.

Next is the masking on and off of the gradient strip, which then becomes part of the main moving map. This graphic/animation is an indication of what is to come next; it also blends into our next scene so the overall sequence is very fluent.

5. To add a new mask to the gradient layer right-click (CONTROL-click on your Mac) and select Mask > New Mask. The gradient strip now has a selected yellow border, and this represents the mask parameter.

6. Now open the mask's properties and add a keyframe to the Mask Shape parameter. Move this keyframe along the timeline to where you like the transition to finish. This will now be the end state of the tween. Press the I key on your keyboard to take you back to the beginning of the selected layer.

7. Click the yellow border surrounding the graphic and press CTRL + A (COMMAND + A on the Mac) to select the entire mask. Drag the mask to the left so that none of the gradient band is left in the composition. Now do a Ram Preview to view your animation so far (Composition > Preview > Ram Preview).

| 0:00:24:23 | | | | | | | | | 0:00s | 00:15s | 00:30s | 00:30s |
|---|---|---|---|---|---|---|---|---|---|---|---|---|
| | # Layer Name | | Parent | | In | Out | Duration | Stretch | | | | |
| | ▷ □ 56 Malfunc 7 | | None | | 0:00:57:13 | 0:00:57:15 | 0:00:00:03 | 100.0% | | | | |
| | ▷ □ 57 Malfunc 6 | | None | | 0:00:55:09 | 0:00:55:11 | 0:00:00:03 | 100.0% | | | | |
| | ▷ □ 58 Malfunc 5 | | None | | 0:00:53:05 | 0:00:54:05 | 0:00:01:01 | 100.0% | | | | |
| | ▷ □ 59 Malfunc 4 | | None | | 0:00:52:17 | 0:00:52:21 | 0:00:00:05 | 100.0% | | | | |
| | ▷ □ 60 Malfunc 3 | | None | | 0:00:50:04 | 0:00:50:08 | 0:00:00:05 | 100.0% | | | | |
| | ▷ □ 61 Malfunc 2 | | None | | 0:00:46:15 | 0:00:46:19 | 0:00:00:05 | 100.0% | | | | |
| | ▷ □ 62 Malfunc 1 | | None | | 0:00:40:02 | 0:00:40:16 | 0:00:00:15 | 100.0% | | | | |
| | ▷ □ 63 Malfunction | | None | | 0:00:59:13 | 0:01:00:05 | 0:00:00:18 | 100.0% | | | | |
| | ▽ □ 64 3D Run 3 | | None | | 0:00:53:18 | 0:00:59:20 | 0:00:06:03 | 100.0% | | | | |
| | ▷ □ 65 3D Run 2 | | None | | 0:01:03:20 | 0:01:10:12 | 0:00:06:18 | 100.0% | | | | |
| | ▷ □ 66 3D Run 1 | | None | | 0:00:59:13 | 0:01:03:18 | 0:00:04:06 | 100.0% | | | | |
| | ▷ □ 67 Malfunction | | None | | 0:00:57:22 | 0:00:59:13 | 0:00:01:17 | 100.0% | | | | |
| | ▽ □ 68 drive | | 46. Grab | | 0:00:24:23 | 0:00:40:17 | 0:00:15:20 | 100.0% | | | | |
| | ▽ □ Mask 1 | Add ▼ Invert... | | | | | | | | | | |
| ☑ ▶ | ▷ Mask Shape | Shape... | | | | | | | | | | |
| | Mask Feather | 0.0 , 0.0 pixels | | | | | | | | | | |
| | Mask Opacity | 100 % | | | | | | | | | | |
| | Mask Expansion | 0.0 pixels | | | | | | | | | | |

The layer mask now reveals the white band. To sync this transition to the audio we must refer to the waveform on the audio layer. Using this, listening to the soundtrack I found a continuous stretch that would fit perfectly.

8. When you click the drop-down arrow next to the mask shape level you will be presented with a graphical view of the mask's speed. The mask needs to reveal quite fast initially and then to slow right down to fit with the audio. Selecting the second keyframe and drag the speed graph downwards to make the mask slow down.

Another way to achieve this is to right-click/CONTROL-click the keyframe and use the Keyframe Assistant > Easy Ease Out or In. Be careful though, this may mean that your speed won't fit your audio, so I prefer to do it manually.

9. To then bring the strip back down for the Malfunction transition, the Mask transition was repeated backwards and the graphic was also scaled.

10. When the reverse mask was half way through its transition, I added a scale keyframe both here and at the end of the masking tween, bringing the graphic down to 5% in height. Combining the two effects gave a smooth transition into the next stage.

11. Once the gradient graphic hits 5% add a 14-frame adjustment layer (Layer > New > Adjustment Layer).

An adjustment layer will affect any layers that sit underneath it. If you were to scale the adjustment layer to 200%, everything else below it in the composition would also be scaled to that percentage.

12. Attach the Malfunction plug-in by Digimation to the layer and tween the speed and variation of the effects to totally distort the graphic.

Watch how the effect pulls the image up and then back down. This effect would be the perfect lead in transition to the map animation.

## Animating the map

The animation process of the abstract map uses layer masking and the Radial Wipe transition. The map was drawn up in Adobe Photoshop, and each element was placed on its own individual layer.

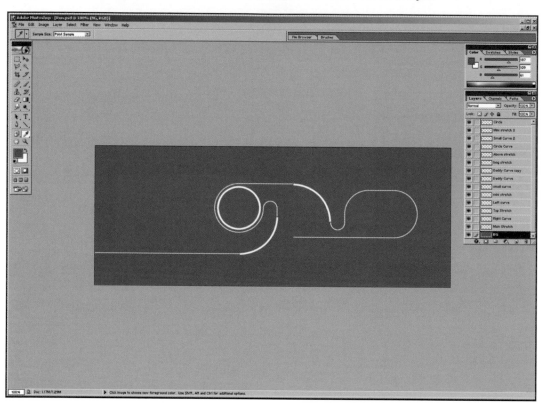

**13.** Once I had imported the PSD into After Effects as a composition, I animated each element to produce one fluent transition. To portray the feeling of the map growing, mask each element separately and time each layer to connect with the next.

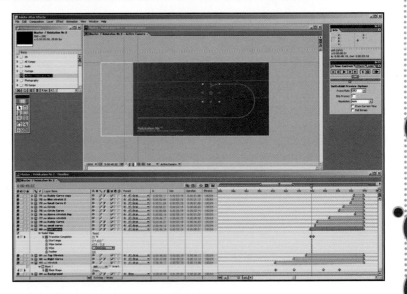

**14.** Use a simple layer mask for the straight lines and the radial wipe for the circles. Each piece of the PSD's layer must connect with the one next to it to form the complete animation. The timing must be spot on for this to work.

By taking each layer and animating them separately, whether it is by masking or the Radial Wipe, the start and end time must be synced with both the first and following layer. For example, the line that stretches the bottom was animated with a layer mask; once the tween was complete the bottom right-hand curve was then animated from that keyframe onwards. This process was used throughout the entirety of the map.

As I mentioned earlier in this chapter, I used the Malfunction plug-in by Digimation to add a static movement effect. I also placed this within certain points of the map's animation in sync with the sound to give the movie a more fluent and formatted feel.

Again, there are a number of different ways to achieve this effect, but I felt more comfortable with this method.

## 3D animation

Relokation incorporates rendered 3D animations at various stages within the movie. To produce the 3D work for the movie I used discreet's 3d studio max. The majority of high-end 3D software can be used for this effect/style but may differ in process. The animations consist of a target camera that follows a simple spline movement within the 3D scene. The look of the spline had to be very flat to complement the style of the 2D map from the beginning of the movie; that way the movie would continue to be consistent.

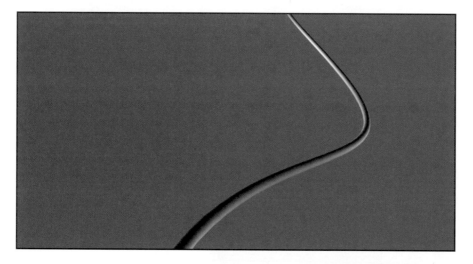

By increasing the level of the 3D object's 3D map all shadows and illumination would no longer appear in the final render. 3D maps are patterns generated procedurally in three dimensions and are overlaid onto 3D objects, thus giving the form color, textures, reflection and more.

I spent some time in 3d studio max animating different sequences and modifying the shape and the way the cameras moved. I wanted to produce as many different rendered scenes as possible and then stitch them together in After Effects. I would render spline movements, shapes growing, spinning, cameras twisting, cameras speeding and slowing down, etc.. Having a library of different movements and shapes gave me more room to experiment and overall added much more variation to the movie.

When it came to rendering each 3D animation I ensured my movies were all rendered as 25fps QuickTime movies with millions of colors plus (+). By rendering out an animation with millions of colors plus your movie then has alpha channels, and when imported into After Effects you can remove or recolor the background.

## 3D transitions

From the end of the map tween the Malfunction plug-in is added once more, but for a much longer period of time. This gives us a segment in the timeline to transition from one animation to the next, but in a fluent and precise way. By setting the Malfunction effect to last over 10 frames, I placed the first 3D render at the mid-point to achieve a smooth cross between the two compositions. Always remember to place your adjustment layers above the components you wish to add the effect to.

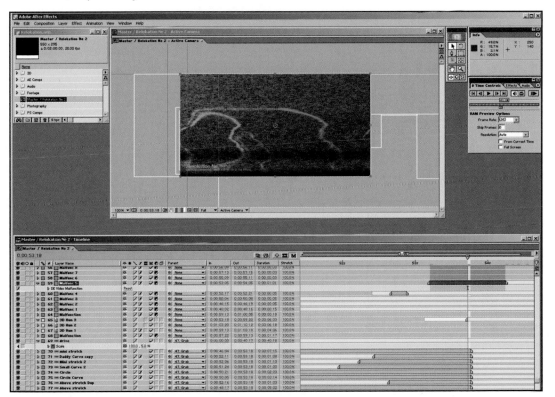

With the 3D animation now in the composition I wanted to visually link the movements of the shape with the overall look and feel of the movie so far.

**15.** Add the Malfunction effect in small amounts to the layer, catching beats in the audio and reflecting this into the sequence.

I added five Malfunction effects to the layer at various different points of the 3D scene. Each one of the five linked up to a certain beat or glitch within the soundtrack. Using this method I could portray a consistent theme throughout the entire movie and incorporate a smooth transition style.

At the 57-second point, I wanted to merge one 3D animation into another, but try and link them up into one fluent and strong transition.

**16.** Roughly a second before the first 3D sequence, place an adjustment layer beneath the two animations to merge.

**17.** By setting the transparency of the adjustment layer down to 20 it can subtly overcome the movie and roll into the next sequence. Then if you add a full opacity duplicate of the Malfunction effect at the end point they merge perfectly into one.

## 3D morph

At the 1-minute point of Relokation the second 3D animation morphs and bends into a different form from its original state. This effect was achieved by using the FE Bend It plug-in. The plug-in can take an object, either 2D or 3D, and bend the entire shape in a liquid-like style.

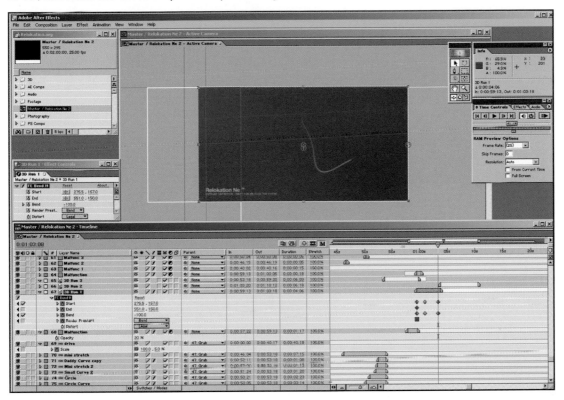

With my 3D animation being quite fluent and smooth already, I was extremely keen to test the plug-in and experiment with different outcomes. Firstly I added keyframes to all the sub-options at the beginning of the second 3D animation. At the 1-minute point I began to experiment with the start, end and bend options until I produced a smooth in an out transition. The 3D spline begins in its natural form and slowly morphs into an elastic interpretation of its former self.

I like to relate this sequence to the ups and downs in life and the way it always changes with every little thing you do.

Unfortunately, there is no URL for a demo version of the plug-in (watch the finished movie to see just what this effect can achieve).

# Bend over

Once the bend sequence was complete I transitioned out into the next 3D sequence.

**18.** Use the Malfunction method used earlier in the chapter. From here the third spline animation is inserted and a fourth overlaid.

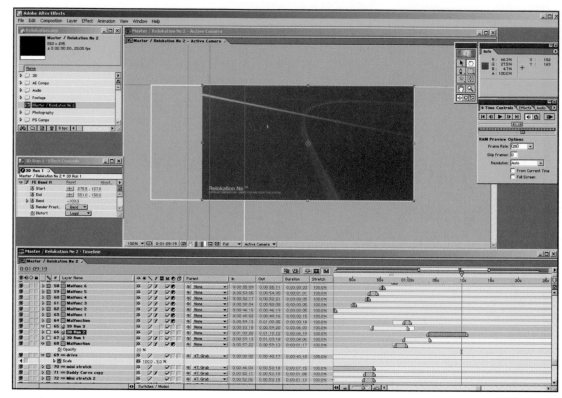

As we have inserted an overlaying animation it now looks like there are two splines animating as one. But the camera has only followed one path, which then leads off into the next scene.

**19.** Throughout all the 3D animations I included tiny static malfunctions in various places, again to sync with the beat and flow more on the whole with the music.

**20.** As the third 3D animation finishes the Malfunction effect is placed over the top and carries the transition into the build of the 3D map. The map was animated in the exact same way as the map used in the beginning of the animation only this time the sequence will be transformed 3D.

**21.** Once the initial masking of the map is complete, place the file in the master Composition timeline for the movie and select the 3D layer tab.

| | | | | | | | | |
|---|---|---|---|---|---|---|---|---|
| ◉ | ▢▢ | ▽ ▢ | 41 🎥 Camera 1 | | 📷 | | ◎ | None |
| | | ▽ Transform | | Reset | | | |
| ◀✓▶ | | ▷ 🕙 Point of Interest | 275.0 , -0.5 , 0.0 | | | | |
| ◀✓▶ | | ▷ 🕙 Position | 275.0 , 556.5 , -298.9 | | | | |
| ◀▢▶ | | ▷ 🕙 Orientation | 0.0 ° , 0.0 ° , 0.0 ° | | | | |
| ◀▢▶ | | ▷ 🕙 X Rotation | 0 × +0.0 ° | | | | |
| ◀▢▶ | | ▷ 🕙 Y Rotation | 0 × +0.0 ° | | | | |
| ◀▢▶ | | ▷ 🕙 Z Rotation | 0 × +0.0 ° | | | | |
| | | ▷ Options | | | | | |
| ◉ | ▢▢ | ▽ ▢ | 42 🎬 **Map Mask 1** | 📷 - ⁄ 𝒇 | ✓ 🗂 | ◎ | None |
| ◀▢▶ | | ▷ 🕙 Position | 275.0 , 147.5 , 0.0 | | | | |
| ◉ | ▢▢ | ▷ ▢ | 43 ▢ Fast Blur | 📷 ⁄ 𝒇 | ✓ ⊘ | ◎ | None |
| ◉ | ▢▢ | ▷ ▢ | 44 ▢ Fast Blur | 📷 ⁄ 𝒇 | ✓ ⊘ | ◎ | None |
| ◉ | ▢▢ | ▷ ▢ | 45 ▢ **Malfunc** | 📷 ⁄ 𝒇 | ✓ ⊘ | ◎ | None |
| ◉ | ▢▢ | ▷ ▢ | 46 🎞 3D Run 4 | 📷 ⁄ 𝒇 | ✓ | ◎ | None |
| ◉ | ▢▢ | ▷ ▢ | 47 ▢ Grab | 📷 ⁄ | ✓ | ◎ | None |
| ◉ | ▢▢ | ▷ ▢ | 48 ▢ Malfunc 16 | 📷 ⁄ 𝒇 | ✓ ⊘ | ◎ | None |

With the layer now as a 3D object I can transform all three axes of the 3D element (X, Y and Z).

**22.** Above the map layer also place a 35mm camera (Layer > New > Camera).

3D layers can be viewed from a number of angles and distances using camera layers. This will give the sequence much more flexibility.

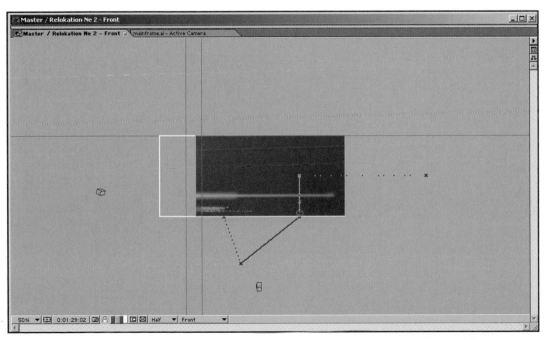

**23.** Add keyframes to all the sub-options of the camera at the start of the map animation and search for a suitable perspective from which the animation can start. Here insert two more keyframes and transitions in different camera views.

In my project, the camera starts off by panning the shape from the side to the middle, at the same time rotating slightly to keep the movements fluent. The camera then begins to track the shape and its growth, and once it hits the bottom of the graphic the map begins to dismantle.

Here I opened the original composition and transformed all the layers to 3D and began to tween the Z position of key elements on the map. Now, as the comp is a 3D layer, the Z position will be interpreted into perspective, thus giving off the effect of true 3D.

At the same time I was also tweaking the position and scale of the map composition to complement the 3D movements. I didn't want to use any motion easing on the keyframes as without they formed a rigid series of movements.

## 3D integration

From this point onwards within Relokation, the movie is built upon using of 3D animations and transitioning from one to another. I produced a series of 3D animations ranging from different camera angles to different forms and shapes.

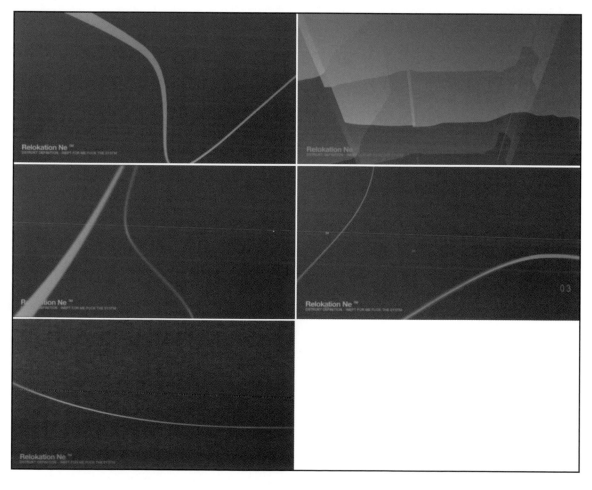

I wanted to cross each animation into the next to give a continuous look. As I seached the end of every movie, I looked for points where they could be linked visually. For example, if at the end of one 3D instance the spline was curving to the top left of the canvas I would then look for a similar angle/pose within the movie I wanted to transition into.

24. By placing the overlaying movie on top the two link up. By adding the Malfunction effect above the two 3D elements you can then forge a smooth and quite natural tween.

## Audio malfunction

At roughly the 2-minute point within Relokation the soundtrack contained a video static sound effect that lasted 2-3 seconds. I wanted to use this area as the final kick within the movie before it reached the end.

25. Insert a 2-second long adjustment layer with the Digimation Malfunction plug-in attached to run over the point when the audio distorts, visually interpreting the sound.

26. Once the distortion has finished, place a frame of blank color to act as a flicker – this increases the initial impact for when the audio and visuals return to their normal state.

## End sequence

For the end transition I wanted a rigid and rapid sequence that was high in impact but yet visually subtle.

27. From the last 3D animation insert a low opacity Malfunction effect and overlay it on top of the movie below. Then, as the audio peaks include a flashing frame sequence that consists of two blank color frames being placed one after another with a small gap in between. From here the audio continues whilst the composition fades to black.

Just when the viewer thinks it's all over the audio kicks back in and the BD4D logo is brought on using the Light Ray 2.5 plug-in.

Before I could attach the effect I had to make the logo into a stand-alone composition so I could increase the graphic's canvas size, otherwise the effect would stop where the boundary box of the graphic size was (Layer > Precompose).

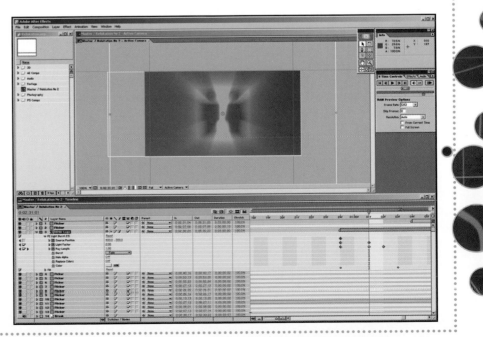

With the Light Ray filter in place I keyframed the position, light intensity and ray length at the start of the BD4D logo. Moving two frames down the timeline I reduced the amount of light and the ray length. One more frame down and I brought the graphic back to its original state. At the same time I also scaled the image down again, not using any motion easing to give off a rigid and hard feel.

The movie then fades to black whilst the audio dies out.

## Relokation Ne™: Overview

My movie holds no secrets and nor is it full of ground-breaking effects, It tells a story. My intensions for this piece were to reflect feelings and thoughts of my recent move to London in such a diluted way it could relate to anyone. I hope you enjoyed this chapter and that it may have caused you to have a surge of inspiration for your next video project.

### BD4D Credits

By Designers for Designers (www.bd4d.com) was set up to bring great new media designers together, at live events around the globe. Its events enable designers to show their work and network with other designers.

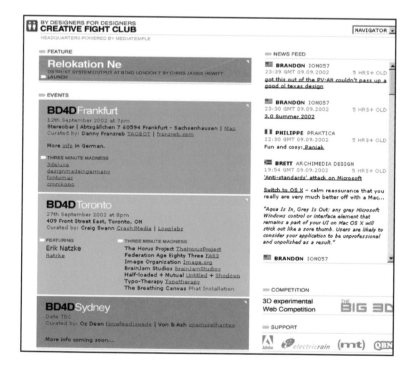

## Production: Relokation Ne™ Credits

Chris James Hewitt: www.dstrukt.net
BD4D: www.bd4d.com
DOSC: www.diagram-of-suburban-chaos.com

Thank you

Joost Korngold: www.renascent.nl
Jason Arber: www.pixelsurgeon.com
Adam Wills: www.dropframe.net

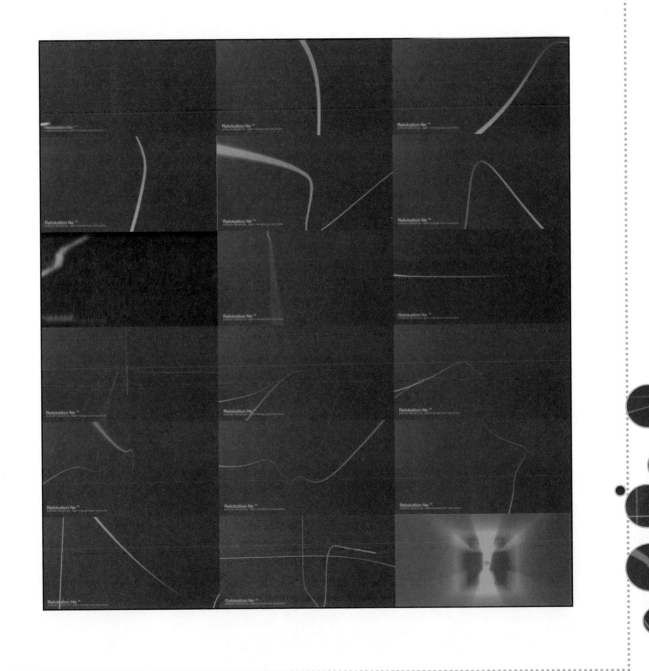

The main reason for me to get into design must have been video games. Ever since I was a kid I've been playing games, from a Nintendo Gameboy to a Sony Playstation 2 now. I've been intrigued by the aesthetics, especially role playing games where the scenery is so beautiful and detailed, with bizarre compositions and perfect use of color and layout.

In school I used to draw a lot. A teacher suggested that I continue my education at a graphic design college as he thought that would be the best way for me to go. Back then I actually wanted to become a comic artist, and draw comics for big American publishers. He mentioned that at this particular school they also had more traditional drawing classes – the combination of both graphic design and traditional arts sounded great to me.

I quickly found out that my comic drawing career would most likely not take off. I've had a few good reviews, although nothing strong enough to build on. That's when I started to take more interest in the graphic design that was taught there. At the time I found it all very boring, too structured "Layout this, type that, use Photoshop like this, use...", well you get my point, I guess.

Then, wondering if I would ever be able to produce interesting work, I was introduced to the work of tomato (www.tomato.co.uk) and the designers republic (www.thedesignersrepublic.com) by a tutor. He showed me examples of their work and said, "Here, this may interest you". I was blown away by their work, absolutely stunning, so different from what I had been taught in school. In a designers republic book I noticed that they were the ones behind the designs for WipeOut, a game for the Playstation. Seeing that made up my mind, I wanted to become a graphic artist and produce work like that.

When I graduated from school, I immediately started working for a web design agency. More companies followed, though it never made me really happy because most of the time I was creating corporate web sites. Only a few companies were making the cutting edge design that I loved since school, companies like The Attik, Vir2l, Kioken and 52mm. There were also personal web spaces from the people that worked there like Anthony (www.onyro.com), from Kioken London, and Jens (www.chapter3.net) who is currently freelancing.

I needed an outlet, some place where I could express my creativity, away from all the rules and regulations. This is when Renascent (www.renascent.nl) was born Renascent means *coming into being, rebirth*. So when I got home I'd be experimenting in 3ds max and Photoshop to make digital abstract art, to later put it online on Renascent. My own little corner in cyberspace has since become a huge part of my life, and has brought me to the point of now being a freelance digital artist.

My inspiration in video games, intros, endings and cut-away scenes in the games lead me into motion graphics. I experimented making little animations in 3ds max and I would edit these in Adobe Premiere although mostly it was purely cutting and pasting and adding some filters. This went on for a while, until I was introduced to After Effects by my good friend Chris Hewitt (www.dstrukt.net author of the Relokation chapter in this book).

Yes! A Photoshop-like application for motion graphics!

After being mainly focused on creating digital abstracts with 3ds max and Photoshop I felt I needed to do something new.

Still loving the digital abstract look the decision was quickly made for my new personal challenge: bringing the abstracts to life by animating them and treating it in the same way as I would with layering my 3ds renders in Photoshop.

5

JENOVAH
Advanced Layering

# Jenovah

I named the project Jenovah. Jenovah is a mysterious evil character from the Final Fantasy 7 video game and I wanted this animation to give that eerie mysterious feel by using digital abstracts and atmosphere.

I will briefly explain the important steps when rendering your scene in 3ds max. After that I will show you how I have used AE in the creation of Jenovah. I will mainly focus on how, with subtle usage of AE, you can get strong effects by giving the 3ds renders more life and atmosphere. And, lastly, I will show how the sound was placed in Adobe Premiere.

The animation is build out of nine main sequences, including opening titles and the end credits sequence. On top of the 7 main sequences small overlays are added, like small text and boxes, though more on that later.

Lets get started!

## Rendering for After Effects from 3ds max

All the footage used for this animation was created using 3ds max. When you render the animation prepared in 3ds max, it is important to follow these steps in order to render it in a format that is easy to use in AE. The key here is the Alpha Channel.

1.  When you choose to render, select either the Active Time Segments or the Range. This basically means that you will render all the frames from point A to B.

2.  Enter the dimension (in this case 380x180), and in the Render Output section, check the Save File checkbox and click on the Files... button next to it.

3.  This opens the Render Output File dialog box. Here you select QuickTime as your output. Clicking this will automatically open the Compression Settings window.

4.  We leave the Compressor set to None so there will be no loss in quality.

5.  Select Millions of Colors+ instead of Millions of colors. This will render your animation with its Alpha Channel!

6.  I set the frame rate to 25fps, because I am working in PAL. Set yours to be compatible with your own requirements.

7.  Then click OK a few times and render.

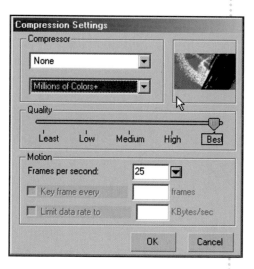

3D rendering is slow. The system I created my animation with is a Dell P4 1.7GHZ with 1 Gig RAM, and rendering all the scenes for this 3 minute animation was predicted to take more than 200 hours.

**8.** As we are going to edit these renders in AE with blurs and overlays, un-check Shadows and Auto Reflect/Refract.

Turning off these options brought a single frame render from over 1 hour per frame to less than a minute per frame.

Also keep in mind that when you're animating, the 3ds timeline has a default of 100 keyframes. As I've set the frames per second to 25, that will make 4 seconds worth of full motion video.

On the CD you will find the end product Jenovah.mov. Also included are two After Effects files that show the layering of the scenes used in sequence 1 and 7 with one frame. The raw 3D renders are over 200MB each and it simply isn't possible to get these to you – but you will want to work with your own particular renders on your project.

## Compo

All right, the time has come to open up After Effects, having prepared and rendered all of the scenes in 3ds max.

**1.** Open a new project and create a composition with the dimensions 380x180 pixels, 3 minutes at 25 frames per second. These settings (frame rate and dimensions) are the same as those set within 3ds max.

**2.** The background is automatically set to white. In my experience this can cause problems when using certain layer modes, so start by dragging a completely black image to the timeline that will stretch over the complete length of the movie to make sure that black background will stay black.

The import of the footage is the next step. As I've rendered the animation from 3ds with the Alpha Channel in the file, we also want to use this of course.

3. File > Import File and select the footage created (I import my first QuickTime file Jenovah1.mov). This will automatically open the Interpret Footage dialog box.

**Interpret Footage**

'jenovah1.mov' has an unlabeled alpha channel.                    △ 0:00:16:21

Alpha

○ Ignore                                                          ☐ Invert Alpha

○ Straight – Unmatted

◉ Premultiplied – Matted With Color

[ Guess ]

You can set a preference to skip this dialog.          [ OK ]    [ Cancel ]

4. The animation in 3ds was rendered with a black background, so here select Premultiplied – Matted with Color, and select the color black. Click OK. This will import the file with its Alpha Channel in place.

5. Now import the same file again, but set to Ignore the Alpha Channel. These imports will be used in the animation, laid under the file with the Alpha Channel. Just how will become clearer in the following steps.

## Sequence 1 – Mysterious source

With the files now imported we can start with getting them into place.

6. First I drag the first scene (Jenovah1.mov) of my animation to the timeline. This is the file where the alpha channel was ignored. I placed the start point of the first scene on 12 seconds from the actual start. I have done that so I can be more flexible with shifting my layers if needed.

If you aren't sure which file has the alpha channel and which file doesn't, you can check this in the overview of your imported files. When an imported file is selected, the alpha channel information is displayed.

**jnvh0.aep** *     [_][□][X]

jenovah1.mov ▼, used 1 time
380 × 180
△ 0:00:16:21, 30,00 fps
Millions of Colors+ (Alpha Ignored)
None Compressor

7. To this layer apply the Gaussian Blur filter (under Effect > Blur & Sharpen). Set the Blurriness to 70 and also add a bit more red to it by using the Color Balance filter.

This will function as my base, or background.

8. Above that layer I will drag the file with the alpha channel in place. With the renders from 3ds some parts may have become too hard-edged. So, with all the imported files, a Gaussian Blur with the Blurriness set to 0.2 will get rid of those unwanted hard-edged parts.

Now that the base and the main shape are in place I will start adding atmosphere over them. This will be a series of actions where I will:

9.  Duplicate the layer with the alpha channel several times and apply Gaussian Blurs. Use Scale, Color Balance and layer modes respectively.

Let me go into detail in the next section.

## Start adding atmosphere

Let's first have a look at where we started, where we are now and where we want to be, as shown with the following screenshots:

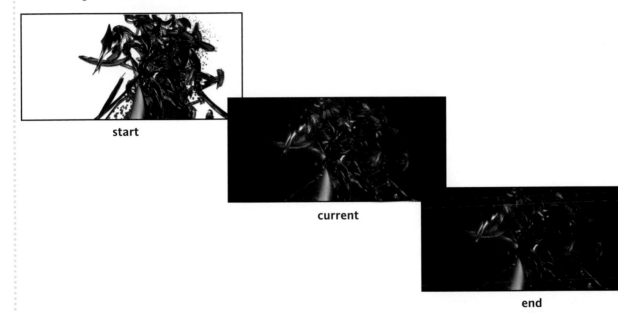

start

current

end

As you can see in the end result, the colors have become stronger, there's a higher contrast and it has more atmosphere around the main shape. All of this can be achieved simply by using that same layer.

10.  First duplicate the layer and use the Gaussian Blur again. Set Blurriness to 12 and the Layer Mode to Lighten – this will lighten up the model. As I don't want it to become too light, change the Opacity from 100% to 75%.

Here you can see the effect the filter has on that layer with the layer mode Normal, and the effect when the Opacity is set to 75% with layer mode Lighten.

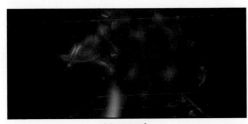

**Normal**

**Lighten**

**11.** Again duplicate the layer and now use Blurriness at 25 to create a wider spread of atmosphere around the model. Then scale this layer to 105% and set the layer mode to Overlay. Let's have a look at the before and after steps with these layer modes.

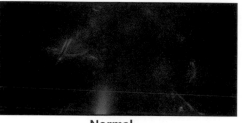

**Normal**

**Overlay**

Overlay will brighten up the colors and contrast, although, when using this layer mode it often makes it so bright that the colors become too harsh. It works especially well with red and yellows. You may like to play around with this to get your desired effect. I've set the opacity to 55%, so it didn't become to bright nor too dark.

The main part is done, though it won't feel complete yet. Wanting to simulate the effect of the camera flying through this mysterious shape, I wanted to emphasize that feeling even more by adding clouds that will blow through the abstract shape.

Earlier in 3ds max I prepared and rendered clouds moving past the screen from left to right and vice versa, as seen in this screenshot. This was rendered with its alpha channel.

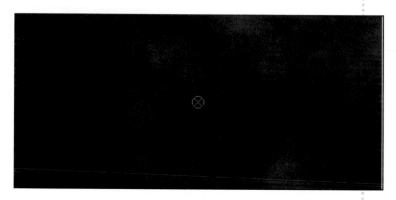

**12.** Place this layer above the main shape layer. To have it blend to the composition, set the opacity to 45%. Leave the layer mode as Normal.

The problem now is having a black and white cloud effect running through the colored scene.

**13.** First add Gaussian Blur again with Blurriness as 3 so that it becomes softer, and then use the Tint filter (Effect > Image control > Tint).

**14.** Tint allows you to have your render/image build with two colors (default is black and white). Select two red variants. The easier way is to select the colors from the model, and then set the Amount to Tint to 100%.

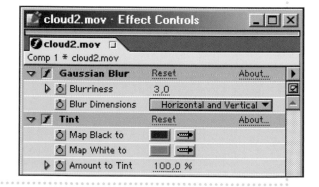

Okay, we can all feel more confident about it now – we have the first sequence finished and the two scenes after that are built in the same way.

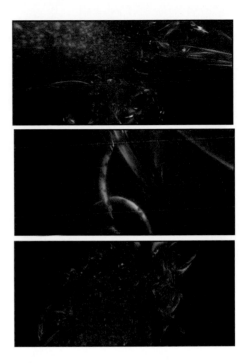

# More atmospheric effects

The process of building the following scenes is mostly the same as what we've just been through. To save time and sanity we'll only go into detail in the parts that make a great difference in our other scenes.

## Sequence 2 - Industrial shine

The following scenes that I will discuss have a lighter colored abstract shape, and are also built of several layers. So, we need to watch how we can use the layer modes efficiently and how I will add a new form of atmosphere called Shine. Shown here is the end result and the way it is layered.

I have layered and modified the files in almost the same way as before. The main difference here from the previous steps is that for the top layer the layer mode has been set to Color Dodge to create a strong contrast and to brighten the colors. This is a great layer mode for accentuating bright parts of the shape. Again, as with the Overlay layer mode you'll need to play with the Opacity to have it blend in as desired.

You may have already noticed in the screenshot that one layer hasn't been selected, though you do see what it does in the final result. It is the layer the makes the light shine from behind the shape. Let's have a look.

## Shine filter from Trapcode

To create this effect I have used a filter called Shine, from a third-party plugin provider Trapcode. If you haven't already got it, a demo version is available to download from www.trapcode.com/products_shine.html.

It is, in short, a stronger variant of the standard Radial Blur filter. I've chosen to use Shine as it is faster and more flexible than the standard Radial Blur – you could, however, use that and get a similar effect.

Let's take a look at the settings that I have used:

- Source Point: this is the center point from where the rays of light will start, identical to using the Radial Blur square field when the Type is set to Zoom.
- Ray Length: the length of the rays, now set to 7. This has the same effect as using the Radial Blur amount.
- Boost Light: the intensity of the rays, set to 10 here.
- Colorize: in my example it has been set to None, meaning that it will use the colors of the layer that the filter is applied to. Alternatively the colors could be manually corrected, or you can choose from predefined color sets.
- Shine Opacity: set to 100%.
- Transfer Mode: none.

What really makes it more powerful than the Radial Blur is that the rays appear seamless and uncluttered; setting Radial Blur to a higher value causes it to generate a pixelated effect. Although this can be fixed by using a Gaussain Blur on top of the Radial Blur it will highly increase your render time.

I will also animate the center of this filter to have it follow the center of the abstract shape. Through the time period of this scene we can place keyframes for certain actions, like scale, opacity and the other standard layer options. Each setting from a filter also has this ability.

**15.** Simply enable it at the start of your scene, and by dragging the playhead over your scene you will follow the movement of the main shape. If you see the center of the shape moving away much from its original center, you simply correct it by pressing on the cross-hair symbol in the source point. This will show a cross-hair in your preview window. Just aim for the new center and click (this is similar to the Radial Blur filter). Automatically, a new keyframe will appear in the timeline.

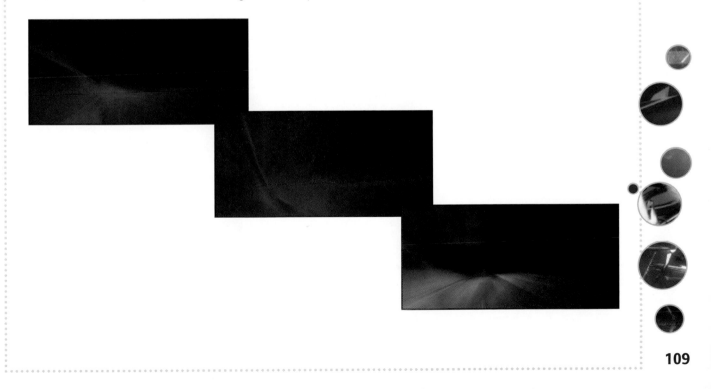

After Effects will seamlessly calculate all the steps between these source points so that the effect will run fluently once it's rendered.

In these Shine effects, notice how having the source point in different locations affects the result.

So we've had a detailed look at the Shine effect, and you can see some of the end results in our movie.

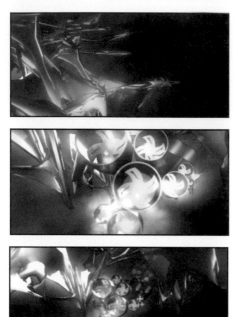

## Sequence 3 - Voices

The third sequence is basically built in the same way as sequence 2. So I will briefly show you the results to move on to sequence 4. Sequence 3 also uses the Shine filter.

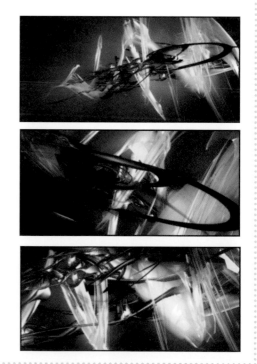

## Sequence 4 - The battleship

I had some difficulties with sequence 4. It is a fairly long sequence (with two scenes) in comparison to the others. Although the shapes were pleasing to me I was afraid that the length could make it a little boring. Therefore I wanted the atmosphere to be intriguing enough to keep you visually interested.

Let's first have a look at the layering in this section.

| ⊕ ◑ ○ ☐ | 🏷 # | Source Name | Mode | T | TrkMat | | Parent | |
|---|---|---|---|---|---|---|---|---|
| ☀ | ▷ ☐ 70 | Layer 1/overlay.psd | O...ay ▼ | ☐ | None ▼ | @ | None ▼ | |
| ☀ | ▷ ☐ 71 | Layer 1/overlay.psd | O...ay ▼ | ☐ | None ▼ | @ | None ▼ | |
| ☀ | ▷ ☐ 72 | cloud2.mov | Screen ▼ | ☐ | None ▼ | @ | None ▼ | |
| ☀ | ▷ ☐ 73 | jenovah17.mov | Screen ▼ | ☐ | None ▼ | @ | None ▼ | |
| ☀ | ▷ ☐ 74 | jenovah16.mov | So...ht ▼ | ☐ | None ▼ | @ | None ▼ | |
| ☀ | ▷ ☐ 75 | jenovah16.mov | Normal ▼ | ☐ | None ▼ | @ | None ▼ | |
| ☀ | ▷ ☐ 76 | jenovah17.mov | Normal ▼ | ☐ | None ▼ | @ | None ▼ | |
| ☀ | ▷ ☐ 77 | jenovah16.mov | Normal ▼ | ☐ | None ▼ | @ | None ▼ | |
| ☀ | ▷ ☐ 78 | cloud2.mov | Screen ▼ | ☐ | None ▼ | @ | None ▼ | |
| ☀ | ▷ ☐ 79 | jenovah16.mov | Screen ▼ | ☐ | None ▼ | @ | None ▼ | |
| ☀ | ▷ ☐ 80 | jenovah18.mov | So...ht ▼ | ☐ | None ▼ | @ | None ▼ | |
| ☀ | ▷ ☐ 81 | jenovah18.mov | Normal ▼ | ☐ | None ▼ | @ | None ▼ | |
| ☀ | ▷ ☐ 82 | jenovah16.mov | Normal ▼ | ☐ | None ▼ | @ | None ▼ | |
| ☀ | ▷ ☐ 83 | jenovah18.mov | Normal ▼ | ☐ | None ▼ | @ | None ▼ | |

The sequence is built of two scenes, and you will notice that there are more files involved. `Jenovah18.mov` and `Jenovah16.mov` are the main renders. `Jenovah17.mov`, `Cloud2.mov` and `Overlay.psd` will function for atmosphere.

When I started, I assumed that using the same layering techniques as before I would get a good result, though I found that the result became rather dull – it didn't speak or attract as much as the other scenes did.

For me the shapes felt like an abstracted battleship. I decided to build further on that idea to emphasize this being a battleship rising up ready for departure.

I rendered a new cloud effect in 3ds max to accompany that, fast flying turbulence like clouds that surround the ship when lifting up was the idea. The render is fairly similar to the first clouds created, though this time moving at 6 times the speed with a more aggressive cloud movement to get a sense of action and power of a battle ship ready for war.

16. Place these clouds between the scene's layers to make the sequence much better.

I then add `Jenovah17.mov` to the scene. Actually, this was a failed render from 3ds max where I wasn't happy about the camera movements. I used this render to create an effect of lights being warped from the lights of the battleship, sort of like a ghost image that appears at random.

17. To achieve this, import the MOV and use a Gaussian Blur with a Blurriness of 16 and set the layer mode to Screen with an Opacity of only 25%.

18. Also apply the Shine filter here as well, placed just above the base layer, to function as a light source coming from above, simulating rays of sunlight that will shine through the clouds.

Once you've put all of this in place the result looks like this.

I looked back on how I layer my images in Photoshop, where I often use the layer mode Overlay to give it more contrast. It really does create a big change in brightness, contrast and color.

Basically what I've done is reduced that layer of the image to the current project dimension and imported this into AE, selecting only that layer from the PSD:

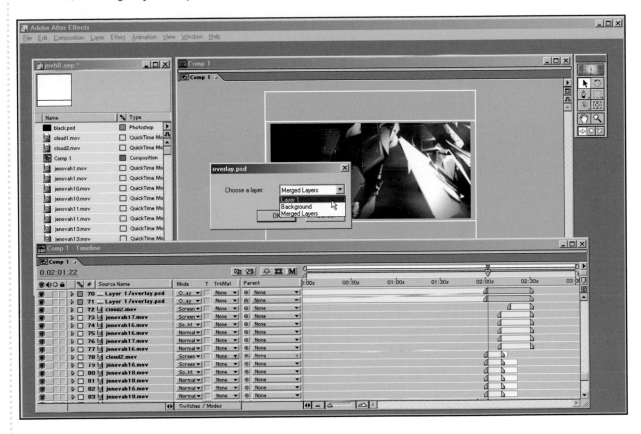

**19.** Place this layer above the all others and set the layer mode to Overlay. To have the layer make an even stronger effect duplicate it.

It is very interesting to see how a simple action of adding the correct static Overlay to your scenes can have such a great impact on your outcome. Shown here is the final result of all the layers used to create the right atmosphere to support the abstract shape.

Here are some examples of before AE and after AE from this sequence:

**Before editing**                    **After editing**

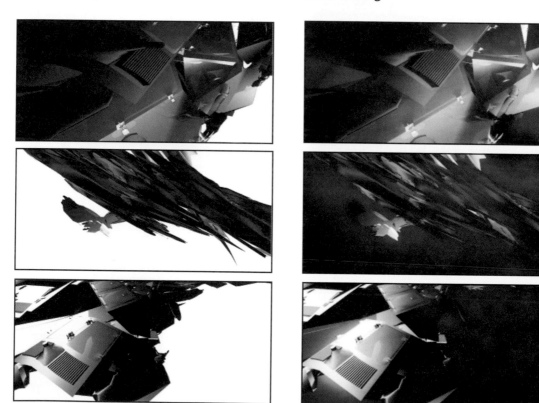

## Sequence 5 - Power beam

Sequence 5 again has the same form of layering, although here I didn't use as many adjustment layers for the atmosphere. The main color of this shape is blue and blue tends to react very harshly to certain layer modes like Overlay and Soft Light or Lighten.

I have used one layer with layer mode set to Screen and the Opacity to 80% and one more layer set to Color Dodge with an Opacity of 50% to emphasize the beam coming from the shape.

**Before editing**

**After editing**

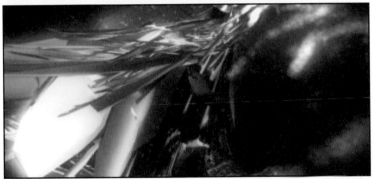

## Sequence 6 - The forest

The render shows an abstract view of a dark forest-like environment with many sharp leaves and branches. The camera moves slowly through it while a source of a small bright light arises.

**Unedited render**

Sequence 6, like sequence 4, was a difficult one to manage. Let me use this sequence to go through all the adjustment layers and actions again.

20. First we place the render with its alpha channel ignored. Apply a Gaussian Blur to the layer with Blurriness set to 65. The layer mode should be Normal.

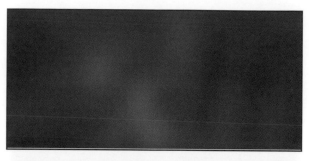

21. Add the render with its alpha channel and add the Shine effect. The source point should be animated to follow and emphasize the small bright lights. Duplicate this layer once to make the light rays stronger. Both layer modes are Normal.

22. Use the same render and apply the Gaussian Blur, Blurriness value 25, with layer mode Normal.

23. Here the abstract shape will be placed with a little Gaussian Blur, Blurriness value 0.2, to soften the hard edges. Layer mode should remain Normal.

**24.** Duplicate the main abstract shape and use Gaussian Blur with a value of 25. Set the layer mode to Screen with Opacity 80% and scale the layer to 115%. Duplicate this layer two times, to make the atmosphere brighter.

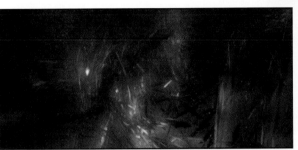

**25.** And the last step is to use the `Overlay.psd` again (was used in sequence 4) to create a more colorful and contrasted rich visual.

Once again this process shows that you can get a very rich contrast and colorful visuals that emphasize the intentions of the abstract, purely by smart layering of two files.

Some more end results from this sequence:

## Sequence 7 – Enlightened fairy dust

The last sequence was actually the easiest sequence to layer – it's only build of 4 layers. It uses the same model that I used for many Photoshop images. The render by itself is already bright and colorful, therefore adjustment layers could be kept to a minimum.

**Unedited render**

**26.** So we set one layer Gaussian Blur with value 65, and the next layer (with the abstract shape) Gaussian Blur value 0.2. A third layer has Gaussian Blur value 12 set to Screen as its layer mode with Opacity 90%. And lastly we add the `Overlay.psd` file to brighten the model and the fairy dust.

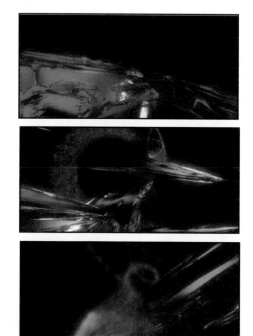

# Rendering the sequences

We're ready to render the complete composition.

**27.** Open the Render Queue (Window > Render Queue) and drag Comp 1 to the open area.

This render isn't to produce the finished film, but will give us a file that we will import back into After Effects. For this reason our render settings need to be as high quality as possible. The following are the settings to use.

**28.** Click on Current Settings for the dialog box to open and Quality. > Best from the drop-down menu. Leave the other options untouched and press OK.

**29.** Click on Lossless, to change the settings for the Output Module. Render the movie as QuickTime format with no Quality loss. Choose QuickTime from the Format drop-down box. Then click on the Format Options button and select No Compression and press OK.

**30.** Leave the other settings as their defaults, making sure Depth is set to Millions of Colors, and again press OK.

**31.** For Output To: click on Not yet specified, enter a filename and press OK.

**32.** Now we're ready to render, so hit the Render button and be patient.

# Adding some design elements

I want to add a few subtle elements to the sequence to emphasize certain parts of the abstract shapes. Keeping in mind that we don't want these elements to become too prominent, we'll overlay these using Soft Light as our layer mode.

The design elements are all white, and by using the Soft Light layer mode, the white parts will blend in with the colors of the sequence. White details on 100% black footage will not be seen if we use Soft Light.

**33.** Make a new composition as we've done at the start (dimensions 380 x 180 and frame rate 25). Import our rendered composition and place this on the timeline.

The design elements are created in Photoshop and saved as a PSD. Each of the individual elements are saved as separate PSD files.

As we've previously done when importing the `Overlay.psd` layer, we only select the layer that we need, so don't choose Merge Layers.

Here are the five small design elements that I will use for the overlays.

**34.** Placing these elements is simple drag them into your timeline and position them in the composition at the desired place.

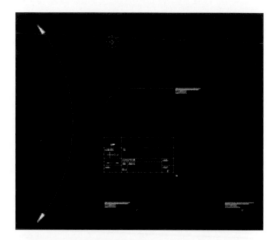

When dragging a static image like a JPEG or GIF, to your timeline, the static image displays over your complete timeframe. As we want to see these elements for only a fraction of a second, it soon becomes frustrating to drag the start and markers of your image, especially when working more detailed in your Time View.

**35.** Cut these files to a shorter time by using Time Stretch (Layer > Time Stretch). In this particular instance I've changed the Stretch Factor to 1% making the New Duration 1:24 seconds from the Original Duration of 3 minutes.

This is how it looks when the elements are placed above the main rendered composition in both Normal and Soft Light layer modes. The overlays blend in in a more pleasing way when using Soft Light.

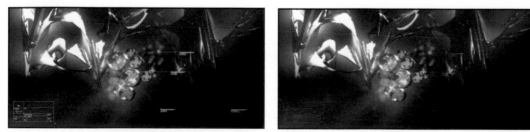

**Normal**                                                    **Soft Light**

I kept on adding these small design elements in the places that I feel need to be emphasized. All durations range from fractions of seconds to a few seconds.

Here are some more examples.

After having added 230 small details, I felt that it was again ready to be rendered to take us to the next step.

36. Now render the composition in the same way as previously described, also making sure that this render has no compression because we are going to use this file again, adding more design details.

So why render the composition if we're going to add more details? I have worked in this way as I felt 100% confident about the placement of the small design elements. Working with so many layers in your composition will drastically slow down your system's performance and will make it hard to quickly modify and see changes made.

You can tell when your composition is becoming too heavy for your system to handle when the preview screen has problems when changing the viewing position over your timeline.

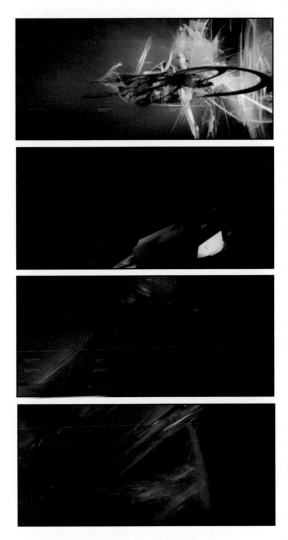

## More design elements

The following design elements are basic blocks made in Photoshop and are larger than the previous details. I wanted to emphasize only key parts of the animation by making these elements appear on screen in an animated way. To do this we'll use masks.

These new overlays will again be placed and their layer modes set to Soft Light. These are the four new design elements. Let's just run through the addition of one instance.

**37.** We first place one of the elements on the timeline. Use the Time Stretch window to make it two seconds long, and then position it.

I want the white block to appear for a fraction of time shown only on the right side of the element. It has to then build up to the left so that the complete element is visible.

**38.** With the Rectangle Mask tool, draw a rectangle over a small section on the right of the element, as seen in the screenshot. The yellow box indicates the Marker.

When adding a marker, a new section automatically becomes available with your marker values.

**39.** Now move the time marker a little bit forward and place the first keyframe for the mask shape.

**40.** Drag the time marker to the point at which the element needs to be completely visible. Now, using the Selection tool, select the mask's top left and bottom left corner points. Drag to the left until the element is completely visible.

Your timeline will now look a little like this:

The preview window will look this. Also shown here is the layer set to layer mode Soft Light.

layer mode Normal with Mask visible

layer mode Screen, end result

After Effects will calculate the steps between the keyframes for a fluent result when the composition is rendered.

**41.** Continue adding more of these design elements until you've covered all the parts that you want to emphasize.

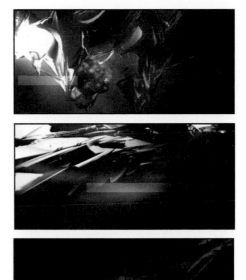

## Start and end sequences

I have again rendered the previous composition and am now ready to add the start and end sequences. This sequence will just be an unedited render from 3d studio max.

At the start it shows my logo being disassembled into particles. These particles will form the title of this project, Jenovah. The particles' movement will be followed by a camera. This effect has been achieved by using a third party plug-in called Particle Studio from Digimation (www.maxusers.com/demoplugins.asp) that allows you to disassemble and assemble the objects that you specify into particles.

The end sequence is built in a similar way, showing the title, the Created By and then a transition to the copyright line.

**42.** Create a new composition so that the start and end sequences can be added.

As I mentioned at the start, I placed the beginning of the first sequence 12 seconds from the start – in order to be flexible with the layers. These 12 seconds of black have remained in all renders.

**43.** Now we place the start sequence renders over it.

**44.** In order to have a small pause between the transitions, I placed screenshots of the beginning and end of each scene that I imported.

The timeline will look something like this:

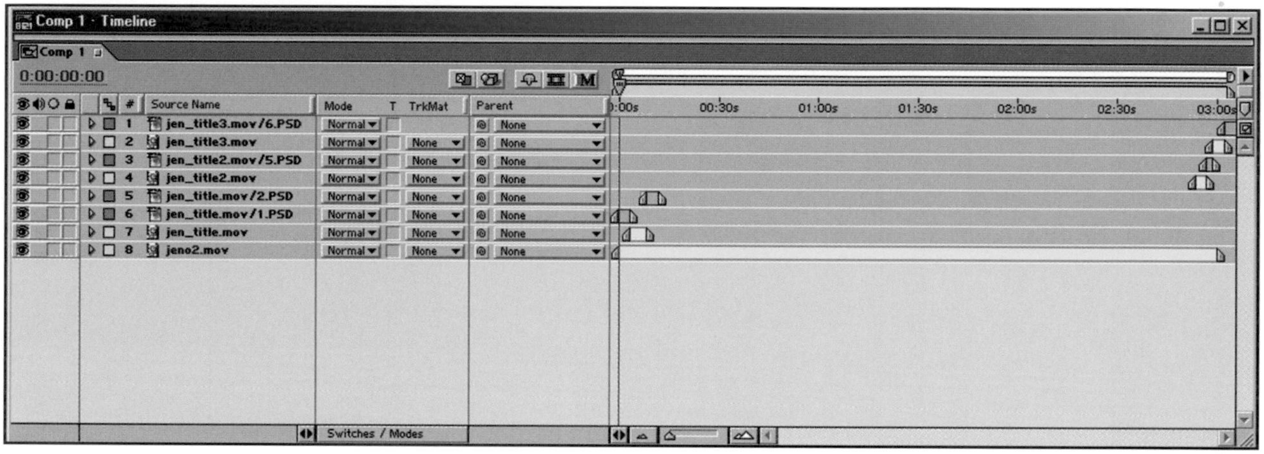

**45.** Ready to render it one last time using AE. This render is also the same as previous renders, with No Compression used.

**46.** Hit the render button and wait a short time to have the now near final product.

I say near final because the animation also requires sound. For editing the sound under the animation I have used Adobe Premiere as I personally find this easier to use when composing to the visuals with instant preview of both visual and sound. If it suits your purposes or preferences there's nothing to stop you adding sound with AE.

I have kept the sound very dark and eerie. It is compiled of many samples that I have deformed to fit the sequences. Shown here is a screenshot of the timeline in Adobe Premiere. It's very similar to the one in After Effects.

With a final render from Adobe Premiere the project is finished!

This render is uncompressed because, for compressing the file, I will use an application designed specifically for compressing movies. This application is cleaner 5.

Compressing the movie with cleaner has reduced my uncompressed render from 926MB to 40MB without losing too much quality of the original file. I've compressed the movie with the QT-CDROM Sorenson High-End settings that can be found in the advanced settings of cleaner 5. I've chosen the Sorenson 3 codec that gives a good quality-versus-size result.

You've now seen the complete process of the creation of the Jenovah project has now been shown. This tutorial has shown you how you can bring your 3D renders to life with advanced layering techniques. I hope to have inspired you to go and jam on your own project.

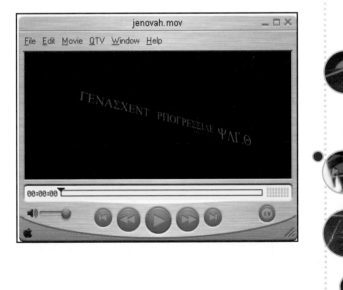

## Special thanks

Joost would like to thank:

Emil Korngold www.clublime.com
Chris James Hewitt www.dstrukt.net
Tom Muller www.ximeralabs.com
Jens Karlsson www.chapter3.net
James Widegren www.idiocase.com
Ashleigh Bolland www.phojekt.com
Bradley Askew www.hellmedia.com
Nathan Flood www.nginco.com
David Rondel www.overage4design.com

for their continued feedback throughout the process of realizing Jenovah.

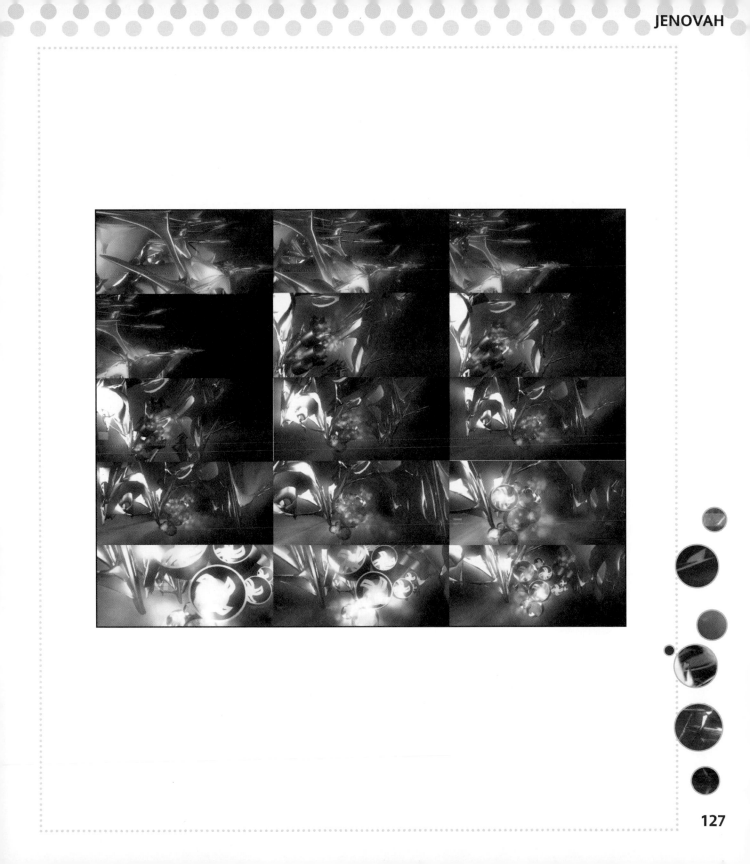

# PETER REYNOLDS

In a general sense, I would have to say I am inspired by anything and everything. Images, visions, sounds, thoughts, experiences, dreams, science, literature, music, art, existence... you get the idea. So, for me, the problem is never where to find inspiration, but how to filter it? The hows and whys of my filtering processes vary from day to day and project to project, depending upon many factors, such as mood, time, weather, and often budgets. So while I'd rather be vague and not give any definitive answer to what inspires me, having been forced to give it some thought, I have discovered there is one thing that attracts me more often than any other factor. That one thing could be best described as innovation.

Imagine what it takes for someone like Nicolaus Copernicus to even begin to think, let alone tell the world, that they had got it wrong and propose that the earth revolved around the sun and not vice versa. Yet people of the time with 'common sense' would have laughed at him or worse, secure in their collective knowledge that the sun revolved around the earth. Common sense is a dangerous term, often used to protect the status quo, and for me, it is the enemy of innovation.

Typogravure published in 1894,
from the painting by Otto Brausewetter

With the development of mass communication and media, some people fall into the trap that, "We've seen it all before". I've even had conversations with a successful motion graphics designer who proceeded to tell me that there was only so many ways you could bring text onto a screen. Try telling that to the likes of Saul Bass (see the outstanding web tribute at www.saulbass.net) or Kyle Cooper (www.imaginaryforces.com), whose innovative work has now become the status quo. Yet each year I am surprised and delighted to see that someone does think of a new and innovative way to bring text onto a screen.

This probably all seems a little heavy for a chapter about a cartoon that is based on a popular commercial film. But, while on the surface the project might seem anything but innovative, what I am striving for is finding new ways to combine 2D and 3D. I am also involved in time-based arts projects, which provide enormous scope for innovation, but for me, a lot of the excitement and challenge is to try and bring some of that innovation into the commercial world. No matter how commercial the project, there are often areas in which you can strive to innovate. I am always actively seeking out those opportunities to try and develop an "uncommon sense".

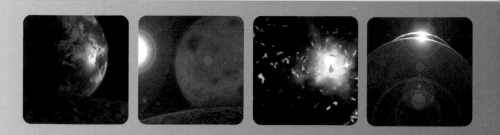

# I'M SORRY DAVE, I'M AFRAID I CAN'T DO THAT

Layering and Opacity, Giving 2D animation real depth

6

I'm afraid I must begin this chapter with an apology. The file sizes for the project I am going to be breaking down are far too huge to fit on the CD, and way too big for a casual Internet download. But I will be explaining the main techniques, so by the end of the chapter, you should have an excellent understanding of the process, and on the CD there are a number of cut down scenes and pieces of the project.

In this chapter we will be working through a segment from an animated short film that I have been working on, titled HAL's Malcontent. The story involves a new take on the misunderstanding that occurred between Dave and the HAL 9000 computer from Stanley Kubrick's 2001: A Space Odyssey.

HAL's Malcontent is very much a 2D animated cartoon, however, what I was interested in was using textures and lighting that you don't usually find in 2D animated cartoons. I achieved a lot of this by painting up appropriate layers in Photoshop, although there were a few shots that just wouldn't work as well without the use of 3D animation and a few particle effects.

## Everything is running smoothly

What space cartoon wouldn't be complete without a huge spaceship fly-by? Which is exactly how HAL's Malcontent opens.

For this shot the HAL spaceship was drawn in perspective. The engine glow and flame effect was created using painted layers in Photoshop. Once in After Effects, a Wiggle function was then assigned to the Opacity to have the engines flicker as the ship cruises by. The engine effects were then parented to the ship and the ship was animated to cruise through the shot. This was then rendered at a slightly higher resolution than required, so if we wanted to zoom in later there'd be no loss in quality. The pre-rendered sequence was then brought into another composition, where another Wiggle function was applied to simulate a subtle camera vibration as the engines rumble past.

### Hal... do you read me

As Dave is stranded outside the ship, a subtle camera move is achieved by animating the various layers. This is possible because each layer was painted or constructed at a higher resolution with this intention in mind, allowing greater flexibility, particularly when scaling layers.

The background layer of stars was painted up in Photoshop. However, individual star layers were also added, in which the handy Wiggle function is again used with the Opacity to make the stars flicker.

A group of separate layers was painted for the spaceship's spotlight so that this could also be animated separately.

## I don't think I've ever seen anything quite like this before...

To achieve a 3-dimensional spatial feel, as the light strikes Dave directly, his protective visor's reflective capacity comes into effect.

I achieved this using a number of painted layers in Photoshop. All of the layers were parented to Dave, and then i animated the Opacity of each layer in After Effects.

To add to the light effects, shadow layers were painted on Dave's face, and a reflection layer of stars was painted to be animated over the visor. Separate shadow and light layers were also animated to effect the whole space suit, including a blue rim light, shadows for Dave's space suit number and highlights for the visor rim.

## Painting with light

It's still amazing how much you can achieve in 2D by simply painting on layers in Photoshop. It's often a lot faster than having to model, texture, light and render 3D, so we're going to take a closer look at some of the lighting effects applied to Dave and his space suit. (See the `hmc_s2_mini.mov` file.)

To make sure these files would fit on the CD for this exercise, we reduced them to 25% of their original size. The reason they were so large to begin with was to allow for close ups and camera movements, which gives the flexibility to zoom in or out from the character considerably.

1. Create a new composition with a Width of 180 pixels, Height of 144 pixels, a Pixels Aspect Ratio of D1/DV PAL (1.07), a Frame Rate of 25 fps, and a Duration of 7 seconds. Call it 'davey'.

**2.** Import the file `hmc_cu02_mini.psd` as a composition.

**3.** Import the file `stars_bg.tif`.

**4.** Import the file `dave_worried.mov`, or instead you may want to use seven seconds of video footage of your own head, or some other victim you want to send into deep space.

**5.** Open the `hmc_cu02_mini.psd` composition. You'll notice there are a lot of layers in the timeline. The reason the file was painted in so many layers is to give more flexibility when it comes to animating the scene.

**6.** Scroll through the timeline until you get to the face layer. This layer is really just a placeholder, so unless you particularly enjoy seeing me stranded in deep space, turn this layer's visibility off. Now drag the `dave_worried.mov` file onto the timeline just above the face layer.

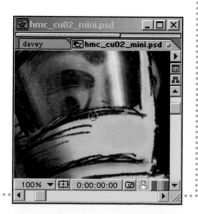

7.  Position the `dave_worried.mov` layer at around 123.5, 102.5. Scale it to 70% and rotate it -13.8 degrees. Dave is now inside the space suit.

We now have most of the elements we need to begin animating. For the sake of this exercise, we might as well start at the top and work our way through the various layers.

8.  Starting with the suit_shadow_rhs layer, move the timeline to around `0:00:03:10`, set an Opacity keyframe to 81%. Then at `0:00:05:00` set another Opacity keyframe to 0%. This should now time nicely with Dave's blink. This shadow layer was airbrushed in Photoshop, and by animating it, we now have the effect of a general light hitting Dave from the right of the screen.

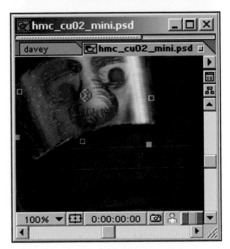

9.  We are using the next layer, visor_stars02, to represent a reflection on the visor of the surrounding stars. Move the timeline to `0:00:06:10` and set a keyframe for 0 Rotation. Then move the timeline back to the start and set a keyframe for +3.5 degrees Rotation.

**10.** Now move the timeline to `0:00:06:24` and set the Position keyframe, then move the timeline back to the start and move the layer down and to the left only slightly, setting another keyframe. This should give the star reflections a subtle drift across the visor. Finally, as the light comes in from the right, we want the reflected stars to fade out and then fade back in as the visor goes into mirror reflective mode. At `0:00:01:00` set an Opacity keyframe of 100%. At `0:00:03:14` set an Opacity keyframe to 20%, and at `0:00:05:14` bring the Opacity back to 100%.

**11.** The visor_top_highlight layer adds some depth to the helmet's rim around the visor, with a 20% Opacity at `0:00:03:15` seconds and another keyframe of 40% Opacity at six seconds. Add these now.

We have another 60% to play with, but making this layer too bright takes away from the highlight further along the right of the visor rim, as you can see here:

**12.** The visor_redstripes_rhs layer gives us the red stripes on the side from where the main light comes, so animate this to increase in Opacity from 20% at the 2-second mark to 34% at the 4-second mark. Add these keyframes and young Dave will look like this:

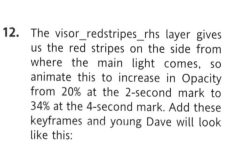

The visor_red_stripes_left layer is not animated and remains set to 24% Opacity.

13. The two white stripes layers (lhs_01 and lhs_02) at the edge of the visor have to be set to 8% and 10% Opacity respectively at the 4-second mark, and animated up to 20% and 24% at 0:00:06:15.

The layers from visor_flare01 through to visor_flare05 make up the bright reflected stripe of light that appears on the visor.

14. We need to animate these layers separately to give a more realistic feeling to the lighting effect. Add keyframes to them as follows:

| TIME | LAYER | KEYFRAME |
| --- | --- | --- |
| 0:00:05:21 | visor_flare05 | Opacity keyframe 0% |
| 0:00:05:24 | visor_flare01 | Opacity keyframe 0% |
| 0:00:06:00 | visor_flare03 | Opacity keyframe 0% |
| 0:00:06:01 | visor_flare04 | Opacity keyframe 0% |
| 0:00:06:04 | visor_flare02 | Opacity keyframe 0% |
| 0:00:06:20 | visor_flare01 | Opacity keyframe 65% |
| 0:00:06:20 | visor_flare02-05 | Opacity keyframe 100% |

A blue rim light is simulated on the shadow side of Dave by two painted layers, blueRim_SAT and blue_rim.

**15.** At `0:00:01:13` keyframe the Opacity of these layers at 4% and 38% respectively. At `0:00:02:12`, set blueRim_SAT to 10% Opacity and blue_rim to 60% Opacity.

**16.** The shadow_numbers layer is another layer put in for subtle effect and the animation of this layer is left to the very end, as this is when the numbers will come into view. At `0:00:06:07` keyframe the Opacity at 10% and increase it to 100% at `0:00:06:21`.

The two layers shade_lhs01 and shade_lhs02 allow us to animate Dave's shadow on the left-hand side of the screen. These are animated to increase the intensity of the shadow as the final light beam reflects off Dave's visor.

**17.** At `0:00:05:18` set them to 96% and 41% Opacity respectively, and increase to 100% and 49% at `0:00:06:10`.

The next layer is the visor_stripes layer, which gives some subtle form and dimension to the visor. This layer is set to 16% Opacity and doesn't need to be animated.

**18.** Now let's deal with the highlights on the rim of the helmet. The layer highlight_helmet01 is the lower highlight, which needs its Opacity set to 0% at `0:00:05:09`, and another keyframe added at `0:00:06:12` where the Opacity should be set to 100%.

**19.** Similarly, the upper highlight is controlled by the highlight_helmet02 layer and is animated to match the light effect from the right, so at `0:00:04:15` set the Opacity to 0%, and at `0:00:05:22` set it to 63%.

You could push it higher, but we don't want to attract too much attention to this to the detriment of the rest of the shot. You will also note that it comes into effect before the reflected stream on the visor, as if the light is catching the edge of the visor before it hits the visor itself.

| ▽ □ 20 🎬 highlight_helmet02 | Normal ▼ □ None ▼ | 🔘 None ▼ | |
|---|---|---|---|
| ▽ Transform | Reset | | |
| 🔘 Anchor Point | 30.0 , 71.0 | | |
| 🔘 Position | 186.0 , 94.0 | | |
| 🔘 Scale | 🔗 100.0 , 100.0 % | | |
| 🔘 Rotation | 0 x +0.0 ° | | |
| ▽ 🔘 Opacity | 63 % | | ◆ ◇ |
| Value: Opacity | 100% | | |
| | | 🔳 | |
| | 0% | | |
| Velocity: Opacity | 53%/sec | | |
| | 53%/sec | 🔳 | |
| | -53%/sec | | |

The next layer down is the no_highlights layer. This is used to hide the other highlights on the space suit, which are painted on the main_space_dude layer below it.

**20.** For the no_highlights layer, we need to create a keyframe and set the Opacity to 91% at `0:00:05:05`, and another to decrease the Opacity to 0% at `0:00:06:12`.

The main_space_dude layer has no keyframes and is set to 100% Opacity. Below it are the three layers that give the visor its yellow reflective shine.

**21.** To support the lighting effect, animate the layers as follows:

| TIME | LAYER | KEYFRAME |
|------|-------|----------|
| 0:00:00:00 | visor_yellow3 | Opacity 10% |
| 0:00:03:06 | visor_yello2 | Opacity 8% |
| 0:00:03:08 | visor_yellow3 | Opacity 12% |
| 0:00:03:10 | visor_yellow1 | Opacity 10% |
| 0:00:03:17 | visor_yellow3 | Opacity 15% |
| 0:00:04:21 | visor_yellow1 | Opacity 31% |
| 0:00:05:09 | visor_yello2 | Opacity 20% |
| 0:00:06:07 | visor_yellow3 | Opacity 21% |

The next five layers control shadows around the helmet, and again, while the changes are subtle, they help add a depth and spatial quality to the 2D animation.

**22.** The helm_shade01 and helm_shade02 layers give shadows across the top of Dave's forehead, and both need their Opacity set to 0% at 0:00:02:13 and increased to 20% at 0:00:03:24.

The helm_shade03 layer simply provides some of the basic shadowing, is not animated and remains at 10% Opacity.

**23.** The helm_shade04 layer gives some extra shadow around Dave's face. Set it to 100% Opacity at the 4-second mark, and then reduce it again to 0% at 0:00:04:14.

The helm_shade05 layer performs the same function as above. It is set to 61% Opacity and doesn't need to be animated.

**24.** The next two layers really increase the depth and dimension of Dave's face and help us with the lighting effect. Animate their Opacity as follows:

| TIME | LAYER | KEYFRAME |
|---|---|---|
| 0:00:03:18 | shade_face_lhs01 | 1 % Opacity |
| 0:00:03:18 | shade_face_lhs02 | 20% Opacity |
| 0:00:04:10 | shade_face_lhs01 | 20% Opacity |
| 0:00:04:10 | shade_face_lhs02 | 72% Opacity |

**25.** To fade Dave's face away completely and show up the reflection, animate the black_reflect layer (which is just a section of black) like this:

| TIME | LAYER | KEYFRAME |
|---|---|---|
| 0:00:04:01 | black_reflect | 0% Opacity |
| 0:00:05:17 | black_reflect | 100% Opacity |

**26.** Finally, to create the general light hitting Dave's face we animate the dave_worried.mov layer, giving it 30% Opacity to begin with, another Opacity keyframe of 41% at 0:00:03:10, and a final keyframe of 90% Opacity at the four-second mark.

**27.** To make sure nothing behind Dave's transparent face shines through, duplicate the black_reflect layer, and move the new duplicate layer underneath the dave_worried.mov layer on the timeline. For this new black_reflect* layer, turn off the Opacity keyframes and set the Opacity to 100%.

This is to ensure that when we add some background stars into the shot, they don't shine through Dave's face.

| 34 🎭 [dave_worried.mov] | Normal ▼ | None ▼ | @ | None ▼ | |
|---|---|---|---|---|---|
| ▷ 🕘 Opacity | 90 % | | | | ◆ ◆◆ |
| 35 🎨 black_reflect* | Normal ▼ | None ▼ | @ | None ▼ | |
| ▽ Transform | Reset | | | | |
| 🕘 Anchor Point | 91.0 , 71.0 | | | | |
| 🕘 Position | 121.0 , 104.0 | | | | |
| 🕘 Scale | 🔗 100.0 , 100.0 % | | | | |
| 🕘 Rotation | 0 x +0.0 ° | | | | |
| 🕘 Opacity | 100 % | | | | |

**28.** To animate Dave drifting away from camera, open up the davey composition and drag the hmc_cu02_mini.psd composition onto the timeline.

**29.** Go to the end of the timeline (seven seconds), reduce the layer to 50% Scale and set a keyframe. Set a Rotation keyframe for 0 degrees, move Dave to the right of the frame and set a Position keyframe for 111.0, 71.0.

**30.** Now go back to the start of the timeline. Increase the Scale of the layer to 100%, set the Rotation to -8.0 degrees and position the layer at 117.0, 120.0.

Dave now floats off into space, away from the camera.

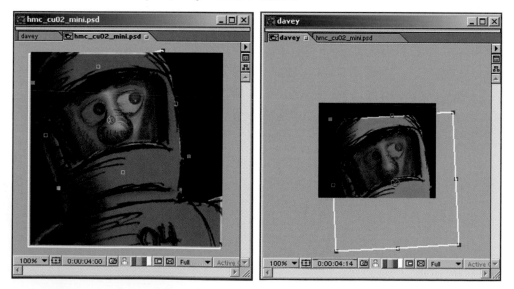

**31.** Now it just needs a background, so drag the stars_bg.tif file under the hmc_cu02_mini.psd layer in the davey composition.

In the original files, the background stars are animated, but, in this case, to save file size, a still shot will have to do here. But we can still liven the shot up a bit more by adding some subtle changes to the stars background layer, particularly given that it is a higher resolution than the davey composition.

**32.** At 0 seconds, set a keyframe for the stars_bg.tif layer's Scale to 100%. Then at seven seconds, set another Scale keyframe at 70% so that the background moves away from the camera, but at a slower rate than poor Dave.

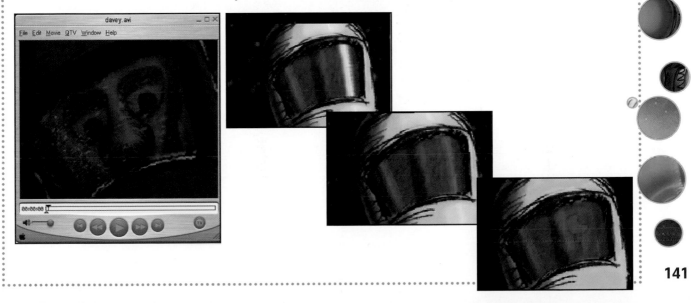

That's it for the shot. You've successfully cast Dave off into deep space. How do you feel, HAL?

## That's a very nice rendering, Dave

Dave was drawn and painted in Photoshop with more than a little help from Painter. The 2D line work and cross hatching formed the basis for his devastating good looks, however he was painted with 3-dimensional shading, with a 2D paper texture applied. In this case, the original Dave drawings were done on paper and scanned in. When it came to replicating the original look, Painter has a number of traditional brush tools and effects that can save you a whole lot of time, and you can save your document as a Photoshop document to bring straight back into After Effects.

It is perhaps neglected somewhat for motion graphics work, but Painter is also a very handy tool to have around. You can actually create animation movie files from Painter, which you can then bring into After Effects to composite. For some of the traditional hand drawn, frame by frame animations, this provides excellent feedback, and in many cases is a little easier than turning layers on and off in Photoshop or going back and forth between Photoshop and After Effects.

Dave was animated in two ways. To save time on re-painting and re-drawing, many of Dave's features were cut up and put on separate layers, and then locked to each other and parented in the relevant order so that Dave could be animated like a puppet. Most of Dave's facial animation, including the lip-sync was achieved this way.

For this form of animation, the only way it can be done is for the artist has to draw each individual movement and then have them played in the correct order – there really is no way around it. There are many books dedicated to animation, and such specialist techniques are a little far away from the subject of our book to get into detail here.

For some shots, individual frames were drawn where a cut-out approach could not achieve the desired motion. These included some facial morphing, arm movements and legs running.

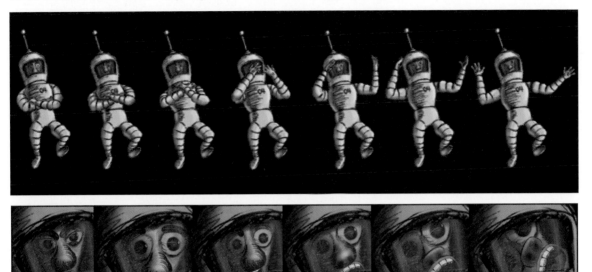

## This conversation can serve no purpose any more... goodbye

Poor Dave finds himself sucked into a mysterious nebula-cum-vortex.

Obviously, the first thing we need is a basic vortex, which you could achieve in any number of ways, from a 3D rendering to appropriated imagery from the Web, or an astronomy book, or magazine. Just be aware of copyright issues, which I've avoided completely because in this case I painted my own in Photoshop.

If you want to be able to zoom into it and not encounter resolution problems, you should make sure that the image is a higher resolution than your composition.

Once the vortex is in the composition and is animated with a slow rotation, the next thing we do is drop our animated Dave into the composite and have him fall into the nebula. While this is a cartoon, it's still nice to integrate Dave into the shot, even though they are painted in different styles. I've done this by compositing a few particle effects over the top, and this helps tie the scene together.

You could create the particle footage in a number of ways, including 3D. However, in this case we used combustion 2's excellent particle system.

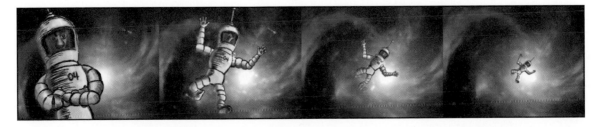

## I can feel it...

As Dave progresses deeper into the vortex, it begins to consume him. For this shot a 3D application came in very handy – that's right, we're using 3D to create 2D and 2D to simulate 3D. By using a simple cylinder and painting up a texture in Photoshop, all we have to do is move a camera through the cylinder and we have the basis for our vortex journey.

This is exactly what was done to produce TIFF sequences. Different render passes gave us different versions, including normal and glow versions.

The two sequences were rendered out a resolution of 800 x 640 pixels, which is higher than the composition resolution of 720 x 576. Why bother with the excess render time? This was done for a number of reasons, including the potential for faking some camera phenomenon such as camera shake, as well as giving us a bit more flexibility for simulating other camera moves.

The Opacity of the glow sequence was animated so that it is 100% whenever a white ring is near the composition's border. At about the midway point between each white ring, the glow layer's Opacity reaches zero. This had the effect of a flashing the glow layer on and off at an increasing rate as the camera and Dave move through the tunnel.

As before, to further integrate Dave into the environment, a number of particles layers were composited into the shot, usually setting each layer composite type to Lighten. Some of the particles layers were also parented to Dave so that they moved with him.

The final effect is a bit of a trip.

# MARK TOWSE

I'd like to let this project speak pretty much for itself, but remember – the projects in this book aren't the important thing, but the techniques. Anyone can copy something parrot fashion, but if you look at what has been done, why it's been done and how it's been done, you'll be a better artist all round, not just with After Effects.

It's not how good the tools are, or how many plug-ins you've got. It's all about your vision and knowing how to make your vision a reality – go to it!

# HORROR OF HORRORS
## Amazing transitions

This project is a little bit different. It doesn't exist (yet), but is a project in motion which will be live and happening by mid 2003. The project is entitled 'Suburban Satan' and is a low budget horror flick that we are heavily involved in (special effects shots, post-production). We are also creating an intro sequence, which is what we are going to show you how to create now. The great thing is that this mini-project is the start of the overall project, and you get to create it in real-time, checking out the reasons behind us doing what we're doing and all the rest.

The project, in a nutshell, is an introductory sequence composed of an MTV style pop-culture smorgasbord that runs along side a music track. Think mass images, rapidly changing with project-related transitions. Should be groovy.

We don't want to risk offending anyone, so basically we will be using a series of more neutral images for this mock up of the project. Don't worry – you can download all the gory stuff (war, torture, death, illness, famine, you name it) from the Bigimpact TV web site, at www.bigimpact.tv. In the meantime, all the transitions will still be based around crosses, pentagrams, fire and the like, as these iconic shapes and images are all absolutely essential to the project. All will make more sense soon!

## Little shop for horror

So, what's the story with Suburban Satan then? It's low-budget horror, but with Hollywood style effects. Thanks to the likes of After Effects and combustion, a good post-production house can do everything as good as the top Hollywood studio – if you have the relevant skills! There is no longer a technology barrier, as long as you are working for DV, DVD or VHS rather than film resolution, which requires a machine (or render farm) with significantly more beef than most people (or companies) have available. This means that we are going for absolute top-level quality. We want the eventual audience to think that this could have been a large-scale cinema release, despite its eventual slightly lower level publication. And let's face it – if it is acted well enough and looks good enough, the sky is always still the limit...

The sequence will run for about 1m 50s in the final project, but we will be creating a slimmed down version due to CD space limitations. (As you know, even compressed video footage is ridiculously large in file size at 720 by 576 resolution – combined with the huge amount of stills and clips required to create the sequence.) Still, all the techniques and transitions will be exactly the same as will be used in the final release.

Initially, we know enough about the film to have suitable ideas to discuss with the director. We have a reasonable amount of creative license, which is always great, but still need to discuss ideas with the producer and director to make sure that what we come up with is going to fit in with the overall feel of the film. Keywords were *dark*, *sinister* and *fast*, as the film will be very much of the modern, fast-paced, fast-cut action that has become a byword in major studio films in recent years.

The degree of creative license we have is directly matched to the relatively small budget of the film, which is good for us, but we have to hit the nail as closely on the head as we can at the offset. We initially suggested a kind of mini documentary, played against a suitable opening music track. At the present time, we are still negotiating the specific song and band. This is within our budget, but we still need ink on a dotted line, so unfortunately we can't publish the name of the track in this book.

However, to give the project the correct feel, you will need (ideally) to be using the right track. You can find the name of the band and track that we are hoping to be using at the following web address – where we will also post the release information about the film when it is finally released at some point in 2003, www.bigimpact.tv/suburbansatan.

Also, please note that when we talk about the music used for the sequence, we will be referring to the aforementioned band and track, not the one we have actually provided (which we already have the copyright to use!).

The director and producer were already fans of the band and agreed that the song's subject matter and feel were perfect for the movie. The track has sufficient energy to combine perfectly with our idea, a rapid-fire slide show of a cornucopia of disturbing images, covering starvation, famine, war, death, destruction, evil, terrorism, butchery, barbarism, crime, bombs, disasters – you get the picture. A 2-minute slide show, however, isn't a viable idea first it's been done to death a million and one times and second yawn... we want this sequence to be the adrenaline rush that sets the tone of the movie and hypes the audience up from the start of the movie. To do that, we decide that the sequence will be filled with transitions and animations of the stills, which will be constantly evolving and changing, becoming more and more complex so that the brain doesn't get chance to focus on any specifics for any length of time; very much like the excellent 'eyeball-open' sequence from A Clockwork Orange, but with motion and interest within the sequence of images. We said all of the above to the relevant people we were working with, and the line was signed – it's always a wonder what mentioning Stanley Kubrick can do for an open pitch!

Please note that for the project you will be creating, you will only have a selection of twenty abstract images to work with, unless you download the 'gore-fest' from our web site, as we want to avoid making anyone sick over their keyboard!

As a courtesy to the people we were working with, we threw these ideas at them and they were all approved. The producer and director were the people we had most contact with, and they had specifically asked that the only name on the introductory sequence would be the name of the film, rather than the usual mass of hangers-on (half the production team and the main actors and actresses etc.), which again meant we had more options than hindrances – text clarity would not become an issue...

After this meeting, we went into production – which is just what we've finished as I write this. This is good for us, as we can simply replace the imagery and copy over keyframes.

Another final point to note is that we have had to make the project shorter for this book, with our final render being about 37 seconds. To create the full sequence properly, you will need to follow the instructions as laid out, creating ten full sections using each of the symbols explained earlier, along with the same sequence of transition style. This is due to limited space on the CD, and the fact that we have used up a lot of our allotted space with the images.

# Start at the end

The final layer will be a bloody pentagram drawn onto the screen, with Suburban Satan text invisible on the screen, as a mask. It will only be visible when the edges mask the flames (from the Delirium package, which has one of the best fire and smoke generators around) flickering in the background.

## A star is born

In production, we started with the only potentially problematic area of the sequence: the ending with the pentagram and Suburban Satan mask and the flames. When this was done, we showed the director and producer and they liked it. Since they trusted us we weren't interrupted until the end of the project and could merrily get on with our job, whilst they did theirs. Everything went according to plan.

1. Firstly, set up your composition (CONTROL/CMD + N), name it 'Satan' and make it 20 seconds long, with a frame rate of 25 fps (of course, this depends on your intended output – ours was for a PAL zone). Make the screen size 720 by 576. OK the settings.

2. Now create a new, black-colored solid from the Layer menu (Layer > New > Solid). Name the layer 'Pentagram'.

Don't forget, you can easily rename anything in After Effects by clicking its layer in the timeline and pressing RETURN.

3. Double-click the layer you've just created and select the Mask tool from the toolbox. Draw a pentagram and alter the points so that it is aligned correctly.

4. Now, from the Effect > Render menu, select Stroke. Modify the size of the stroke (width) and the color, so that you have a reasonable thickness and a nice dirty red color. We have used Maya Paint Effects (www.aliaswavefront.com) with the Red pastel setting, but an After Effects Stroke will give exactly the same effect.

5. Now apply Effect > Perspective > Bevel Alpha, with the Edge Thickness set to 4.

**6.** Scale the pentagram down by double-clicking the pentagram mask that you created and drag-selecting all the points on the star. You will see the yellow mask over the top of the pentagram – to remove this, simply click off screen. Make sure the pentagram is scaled to about the size of the one shown in the screenshot, and also make sure that it is centralized.

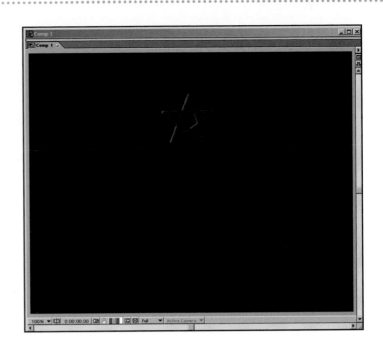

## Burn baby, burn

Now for the real fun. We need to create a realistic field of smoke and flames, with an emphasis on the flames. Our plug-in pack of choice, Delirium (www.digieffects.com/index2.html), contains what is simply one of the best 2D, non-particle based fire generators there is. It can be a bit mean on the render times, but for realism you can't beat it

This may be a wise point to turn the resolution down to a half or quarter and the quality to low, depending on how powerful your computer is. This will allow you to view the makeup of the flame prior to rendering without destroying your workflow by waiting for screen refreshes.

**7.** Create a new black solid, called 'fire'. Drag the layer to the bottom of the stack in the timeline, so that the pentagram layer remains visible. In the Effect menu, select DigiEffects Delirium > DE Fire.

You should have a nice blob of fire in the center of your screen.

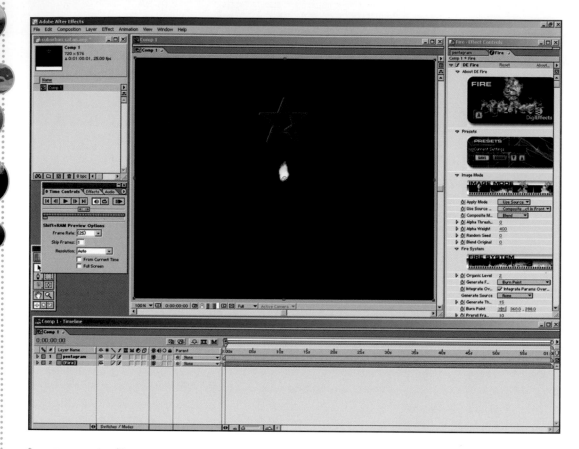

8.  Import the file Mask.tif from the CD-ROM. Click Guess, when prompted, and turn on Invert Alpha.

9.  Drag the mask to the timeline and turn off the layer's visibility by clicking the eye icon in the timeline. If you can't see this icon, you may have to click the Switches/Modes tab at the bottom of the timeline.

The mask you have created will be used as the generation source for the fire layer, so there will be flames of different sizes all over the rectangular mask. After this, we will create a layer with Suburban Satan typed in Basic Text, and use an Alpha map to let the flames flicker through.

**10.** Select the fire layer, and open the effect settings. You need to change Generate Source to Mask.tif. You must also change the Generate From setting to Generate Layer Alpha > Threshold. You will see the fire is now generated from the rectangular mask of the TIFF file.

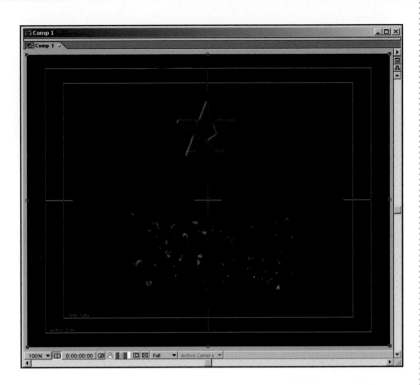

Now the task is to change the flames from the slightly pitiful mini-blobs that litter the screen at the moment, and make them look real.

**11.** Change the following settings within the DE Fire effect. Firstly, change Organic Level from 2 to 4. This creates two extra layers, using the same settings but slightly modified. It increases render times, but is most definitely worth it.

**12.** Increase the flame's Min Size to 60 and Max Size to 130, for some larger flames.

**13.** Now copy and paste the entire layer, and modify the settings again. This time, reduce the Organic Level back to 2. Change the flame Min Size and Max Size settings to half of their previous values. Increase Flame Lifetime to 65. Change Random Seed to 4.

**14.** Make sure the layer is dragged just above the original fire layer, and click the Switches/Modes tab at the bottom of the timeline. For the copied fire layer, select the Screen blending mode. The fire is looking richer already.

Now, be warned. Ideally, you will use a further two modified layers and pre-composite them together to make a good quality realistic fire. This, as you may have realized from the other two layers, takes an age to render. I recommend leaving the fire as is for now, and adding some extra layers when the project is finished, for that extra little bit of pizzazz.

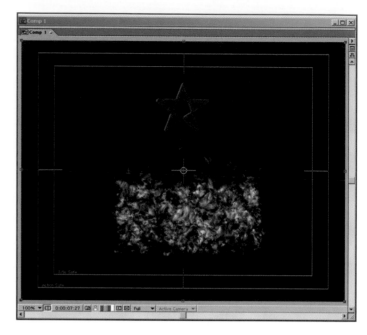

**15.** Now, create another new solid layer, called 'Satan text', and apply the filter Basic Text (Effect > Text > Basic Text). Type 'Suburban Satan' in a suitable font – we have gone for the chunky Impact font, which will allow more of the sea of flames to flicker through.

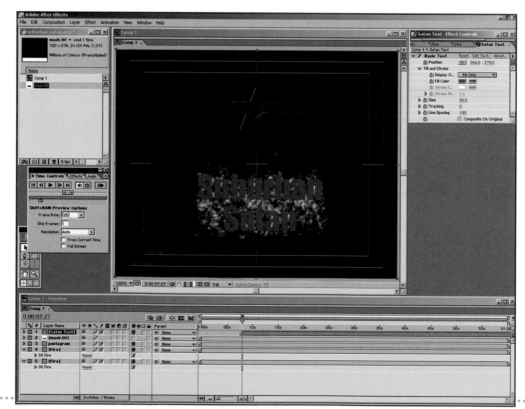

**16.** You must position this layer at the bottom of the timeline stack. Select the two fire layers and press CONTROL/COMMAND + SHIFT + C to pre-compose. These two layers are now above the text layer, combined into one composition.

**17.** Now make sure that you are still in the Modes section of the timeline, so we can turn the text layer into a Matte.

Again, for the sake of speed it will actually be much more efficient to delete one of the fire layers and re-add it at the end of the project, as the extra speed we can operate at now more than outweighs the temporary loss of detail on the image.

If we simply make a Luma or Alpha Matte, the fire underneath loses its rich flame-like color (do give this a try and see for yourself), so we actually need to create a mask directly on the layer to let the flames show through with all their richness and realism.

**18.** For this, simply draw a mask directly onto the text layer. With a thick font, this only takes a few minutes.

You won't see anything happen to the layer, because you now need to turn off the Basic Text effect.

**19.** To do this you don't invert the masks you created, but change the mask mode from Add to Subtract for the outer masks. For letters like 'B' and 'A' keep the mode to Add, to maintain the interior region which gives the letter its detail.

You can now see where we were going with this mask manipulation, and when the extra layers of flame have been added you get an incredibly rich bubbling lake of fire underneath the Suburban Satan text.

Now return to the pentagram layer. We wanted to animate the drawing of the pentagram, but we fancied making the drawing a little different – as always! We would draw from the center of the cross line, both left and right at the same time, so that we can have the ends meeting in the center of the top star point.

It is a wise move to turn off the fire layer temporarily.

**20.** For this, click on the pentagram layer and press E to open the Effects window. On the Stroke effect, make two keyframes for the stroke start and stroke end.

**21.** Press U to remove all keyframeable options other than the ones you have applied keyframes to. Drag the stroke start and stroke end slider in the timeline so that the two directions of stroke both start from the middle of the layer. This value will depend on how you drew the pentagram in the first place. We started from the top middle, so both of our values are 0.510. This will be different for everyone, and isn't difficult to figure out.

**22.** Now add another keyframe at 4 seconds. Keyframe the values so that the Stroke effect animates the drawing of the pentagram. Your ending values should be 0 and 1 respectively.

**23.** You also need to animate the Bevel Alpha setting, so that it grows from 0 to 4, starting at the end of 4 seconds and finishing its growth at 6 seconds.

This is because even though the Stroke effect is not actually on screen at the start of the stroking process, the computer sees it as being there but not visible, so the Bevel Alpha is applied to a 'ghost' of the pentagram. By animating in the suggested fashion, you remove the telltale ghost edges of the Bevel Alpha effect.

**24.** Now, you must also animate the Opacity of the fire layer, starting at 0 seconds with 0% Opacity and ending at 6 seconds, with 100% Opacity. The keyboard shortcut is CONTROL/COMMAND + T.

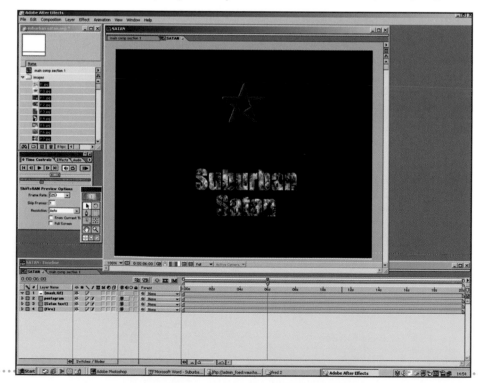

**25.** Now it's time for the final touches. Select the Satan Text layer, with all the masks, and apply the Effect > Render > Stroke filter (not the Maya Paint Effects one).

**26.** Select All Masks in the Effect Controls window, and make the stroke 1 pixel wide (Brush Size = 1), with a subdued yellow color. Keyframe the stroke start to begin with 0% at 0 seconds, and to finish at 6 seconds with 100% completed.

With the All Masks setting selected, the masks will be drawn in stack order in the timeline, so it is useful to re-jig the stack if, (like me) you copied and pasted many of the masks to save time earlier. This will give the edges some purchase when the extra layers of fire overwhelm the masks later on, and also line up with the Bevel Alpha effect on the pentagram.

**27.** The entire part of the project we have just created now needs pre-compositing, so we can drop it into the end of our main sequence as we see fit. Select all the layers and press CONTROL/COMMAND + SHIFT + C. Name the composition 'Final sequence'.

Perform a test render if you like – it looks even more impressive with the extra fire layers!

## Creating the sections, transitions

We agreed internally that it wouldn't be creatively prudent to have the barrage of images hitting the audience from the start, and that a slow, methodical build up to the climax of the piece would be better. The climax will be images too fast for an individual brain-fix, combined with a final slow-motion clip of the nuke going up at Hiroshima.

The music, which has a sparse start followed by particularly hard and fast riffs, would fit best to a blank screen with the volume fading up until the 'beef' begins. The music's slowish build up, followed by some heavy base, can support one image on screen for a short length of time, before the build up to the rapid-fire documentary element. This would be suitable for our requirements as we weren't keen on the idea of having a linear increase in the speed and complexity of the imagery we would use. This will simply lead to a boring first 45 seconds followed by things getting too nuts for the remaining half of the sequence; clearly no good for the audience. So, as soon as the main riffs begin, we were going to go for the jugular, as in time to the music as we could possibly make it.

As you know, transitions are simply different erosions of an image that overlaps another. Normally, you get cross-fades, Venetian blind wipes, circular wipes and a myriad of others. Certain imagery would be useful for certain types of transition, such as the image of a rocket launch being good for a rapid vertical cross-fade, but, for the most part, we wanted to stay away from the kind of standard transitions that you expect to get as part of any low cost editing package.

Fortunately, transitions can be highly complex and also follow bespoke grayscale patterns, meaning that we were not tied to anything as dull as the above suggests. To get the most of our transitions, we had to employ the services of a few old plug-in buddies.

We will be using many of After Effects' own inbuilt transitions and filters, but for several specific effects we need outside help. Fortunately, fully working versions of all the demos are available for free download, meaning you won't miss out on a trick.

The main one we're going to use here is SpiceMaster from Pixelan (www.pixelan.com/download/form.htm). This is the most comprehensive transition package I have yet come across, and allows you to choose from a few thousand different transitions with a multitude of keyframeable attributes. Clearly, for a project so reliant on transitions, this was going to be a must. The other big selling point for us is the fact that you can use your own grayscale maps to create transitions. This means that if we take a grayscale image of, say, some fire (or more accurately, an image of fire, desaturated in Photoshop and with contrast improved so the lightest color is white, but the darkest gray is turned to black) we can then use SpiceMaster to keyframe a new and unique flame transition. Invaluable.

Okay, so with transitions taken care of, we didn't need much else – but I remembered one transition I had worked with a long time ago, from the excellent Delirium package from DigiEffects. FlowMotion was its name, and it uses some hefty algorithms to not just wipe or erode one image, but to use the RGB values of both the top and bottom images to mix together to create some excellent fluid warps and transitions, which are murder to create manually. This meant that we could even use default settings for a good portion of the imagery, saving a load of time and adding another swish effect that is hard to tire of.

With these plug-ins and the music we were a few steps closer to our goal. However, we still wanted to make sure that we had enough interesting movements, zooms and masks, and other sneaky tricks within After Effects to make sure we were (are) not still completely dependent on pure usage of transitions from these packages. This meant that we would have to have a look at After Effects itself for some groovy effects that we could mix up and add some interest to the final look of the sequence. One idea was to split channels occasionally, so the RGB (or HSL, depending on the tones used on the image!) were scattered, and being pulled together to create a recognizable image. Another was for us to use Maya Paint Effects images such as pentagrams, upturned crosses and the like, and then zoom into one of the star points to reveal another image on a layer below, which would already be mid-stroke on a cross, which we would spin and zoom into, revealing another sequence of images and so on. This seemed like an ace way to keep movement on the screen, whilst still using the transitions – and the zooming images were very useful to give a feel of extra depth to the piece.

When we saw this, we got the next big brainwave for the rest of the project. We would be using multiple layers, and, from the outset, there would be clusters of imagery that got progressively more repulsive and disgusting, depending how far down the layer stack you were. This meant that we could warm the audience up slowly with only semi-disturbing imagery and slower transitions, and use the tracing on the screen of various film-relevant symbols to cut holes in the imagery and zoom through to the next faster, harder and more disturbing layer, until we finally made it to the end layer.

After this, the Bigimpact posse all sat around fervently listening to the music to identify key points at which we would 'stroke and zoom', as it were. This was surprisingly tricky, as, other than the music, we had no reference points, and everyone had different ideas on what would constitute a good point for the different sections of the project to come into play. In the end, the buck stopped with me and I went for a kind of compromise. We would have progressively shorter sequences with a final very fast barrage before the fire Satan flames were shown on screen.

We would like to thank up and coming unsigned band Malousche for allowing the use of a sample of one of their tracks, 'Highland Cattle', on the CD, although we still aim to get the track we spoke about earlier. Fortunately, the tempo and style of the track isn't a million miles away and will thus make a pretty good stand in!

After this was completed we did a few mock-ups of how the traced strokes would appear on screen, and also which symbols would be the basis for these. We went for a cross, an inverted cross, a pentagram, the Star of David, an outline of a devil's head and a swastika. This gave us six, and we would use them twice for a total of twelve distinct sections of progressive violence and general horribleness. Given the overall sequence would be slightly under 2 minutes (again, we were lucky that there was a bit off leeway in this respect), we had no problem with this amount of sections. It meant we could start off with the basic sections being around 10 seconds long, and each consecutive section being about 1 second shorter. This meant we would have time to fade up from black at the start, and have about 20 seconds for the traced pentagram to appear at the end and leave there as we hear the tumultuous climax of the song.

The actual transitions within the sections were a much more hit and miss affair. Some transitions would lend themselves to specific images very easily, and some wouldn't. We would just have to try and mix the transitions already in SpiceMaster, the ones we would custom create and the FlowMotion transitions together to fit as well as possible. The only proof of this pudding would be in the eating (or checking test renders) and a good healthy dose of animator's intuition.

We also decided at this point that we should keep the type of transition roughly in the same sequence for each of the consecutive sections. This was so that we could get a feel of continuity to the chaos, and so that as the clips and transitions got faster and faster it would generate a kind of cyclical, hypnotic repetition which would look very good when combined with the disturbing material we were to use. And creatively, that was that – only the graft to do now...

1.    Create a new composition, this time 10 seconds long. Set the frame rates and so on as you did for the previous composition. Import the audio file `Highland Cattle.wav` from the CD. Also import all the `I1`, `I2`, `I3`, and so on, JPEG image files, which are in the images for use in project folder.

There are 22 for you to use here, but you can find the 100+ actually used in the project at the Bigimpact TV Ltd web site, www.bigimpact.tv. They are gory, they are offensive – you have been warned.

Make sure you organize your files in the project window by creating separate folders for images, audio, and compositions - you'll struggle later if you don't.

2.    Drag all the image files to the timeline.

For this stage we just want to throw everything in the melting pot together and add all of our transitions. After we have done this we will sort out the zooming layers, adding the music and adding some other effects to keep the piece interesting.

3.    With the first layer selected, go to the Effects menu and select Pixelan > SpiceMaster.

**4.** We actually want to be able to view the transitions we want to use, rather than use the default cross fade setting. Click the Options, option in the Effects Control window and you will see a real-time graphical representation of the transition you are using.

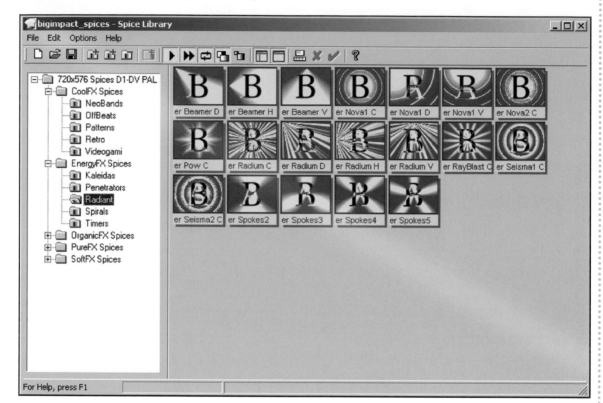

This section is a little deceiving. You will get a transition of the style you see, but we will be manipulating the effect's edges, softness, shadow and the rest to make the transitions look very different, but at least the menu gives you a good general idea what to expect.

At this point, please be aware that you can chop and choose as you see fit, as we aren't using the original soundtrack or the proper 'evil' static images. Use what I am writing as a guide to see how to achieve a certain effect, rather than an absolute keyframe here, animate there kind of scenario.

**5.** I have applied ER Radium H from the Radial section as a starter. You will notice that absolutely nothing has happened. We must keyframe the amount of the transitions that has been completed. Set a keyframe at the start of the timeline on the Completion setting, and a further one at 1 second with the Completion set to 100%.

If you move the timeline head to half a second, you will see the transition half way through. Okay, quite fine –
but a bit, well, transitiony

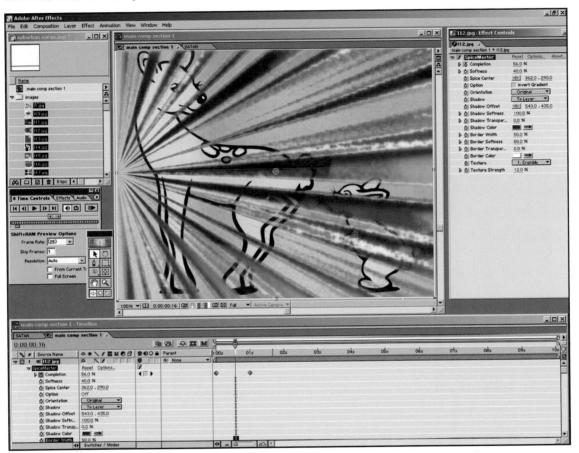

6. To heat things up a bit, change the Effect Controls settings to a Softness of 40 and the Shadow to the To
layer setting with a Shadow Softness of 100%. Set the Border Width to 50% and the Border Softness to 80%.
Leave the default Texture of Crumble, and set the Texture Strength to 12%.

Now things are looking a bit more interesting. Drag the slider so that you can see what is happening. What makes
SpiceMaster so powerful is that all elements, including borders, textures, softness, shadows – the works – can all
be animated, so the plug-in acts as much more than a transition kit and more like a whole effects suite of its own
unique variety.

7. Move the second keyframe back from the 1-second mark and put it at the half-second mark.

8. We need to keep things tidy, so drag the top layer's cropping triangle to the end of the second keyframe.

9. Now select the second layer and add another spice, following the same pattern as before. We have opted
for a creeping cross fade, OL Eroded 1H from the Organic FX spices selection. We used a Softness of 30%
to give a kind of 'Scooby Doo' creeping cloud effect.

We didn't use any shadow or border controls on this layer, remembering the After Effects golden rule: just because you have 5,000 settings and 20,000 extra plug-ins, they are all there for a reason and don't need to be used for the sake of it.

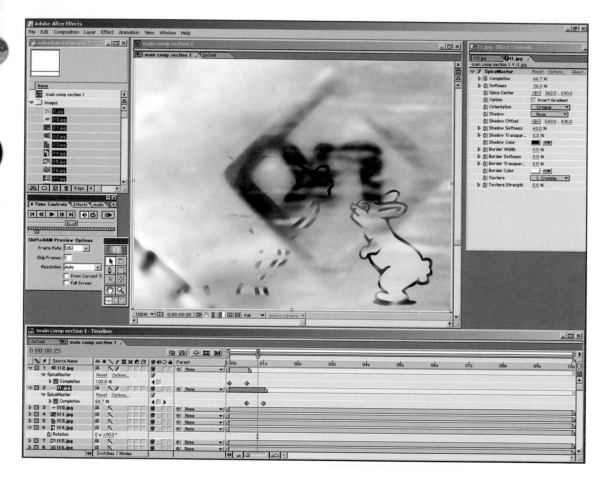

10. Again, move the cropping triangle to the end of the keyframe, which makes any future modifications much easier, as you have an immediate reference point for the layer you are working on.

You kind of get the idea (I hope!) by now. So repeat these steps several times, not forgetting to keep the transitions different and interesting. I would love to explain what we did to each transition individually, but that amounts to about 100. Simply remember to cycle the transitions every 5, 10, or a figure that suits you. We were specifically going for every 10 so that there is a sense of repetition, despite the rapidly changing images.

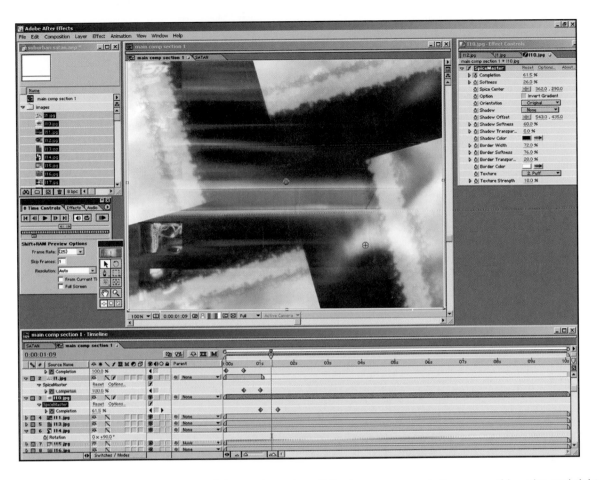

11. Work your way to the bottom of the stack, so that all the images are used. Keep everything nice and tight, and do a test render.

12. Now create a new composition.

We will be nesting consecutive compositions so that we can use the transition elements with our other effects and our 'symbol strokes'.

13. Overall, you must create ten of these sections, ideally downloading the extra elements from our web site or adding images of your own. If you don't, you will have to use repetitions of the twenty-two images, as we have done due to CD space limitations.

Each section, remember, should be a second shorter than the last, and have a very slightly faster transitions each time, building up the tempo through each of the sections.

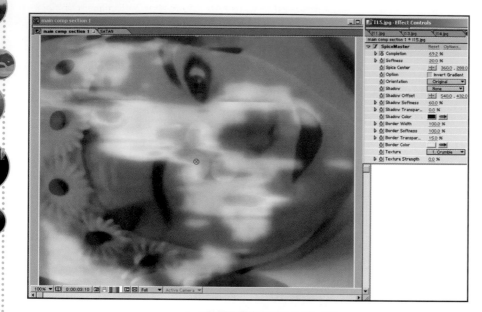

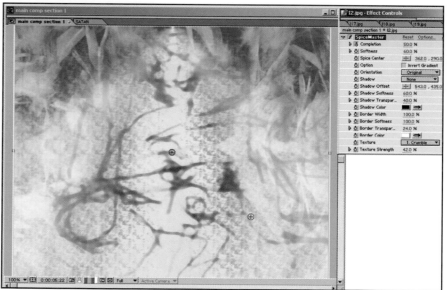

## Creating your own transitions

As promised, we wanted to move away from completely pre-created transitions, no matter how many variations we introduced.

**14.** So, whip yourself off to Photoshop, Paint Shop Pro or similar and create a new image, 720 by 576 (or the same size as your composition).

We want to create a grayscale image. Easy enough, but to make a transition you need to know that the transition engine (SpiceMaster in this case) is looking not at pictures and patterns, but the lightness of the pixels. It begins at black and moves down to white, covering 255 different values of gray in the middle.

**15.** This means that to get a transition that, for example, looks like a swastika, the first step is to draw a black and white swastika. That's what we've done for the real project — here we've drawn an abstract 'x' (in Photoshop 7).

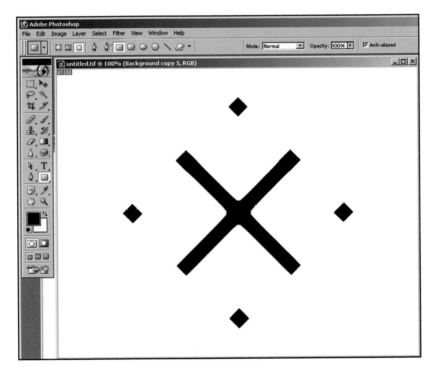

**16.** Now we want to add a small blur that completely surrounds the symbol we want to turn into a transition.

**1.** To achieve this in Photoshop, copy your background layer. If necessary, get rid of a white background by clicking once with the Magic Wand tool and pressing DELETE. With that done, apply a Gaussian Blur (of about 20 pixels) to your new layer

**2.** If you want to darken your layer, duplicate it. Because it's got a clear background, this'll have the effect of duplicating the darker areas and so make the blur seem 'closer' to the object.

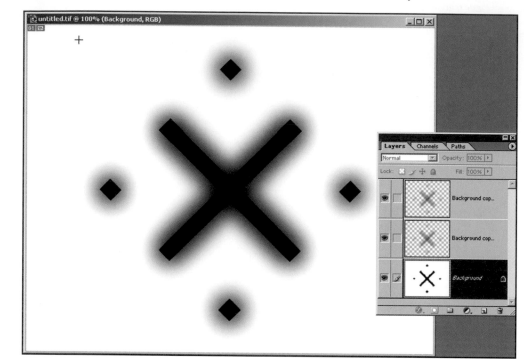

**3.** Now merge the layers and save as a BMP.

**17.** All you have to do now is save the file into the folder that contains the other 'spice' grayscale images, and you're done. For a smoother finish, putting a very slight white to light gray ramp from the edges of the image to the center will do the job perfectly.

You must be sure to save as an 8-bit image, or you won't be able to use your new transition within After Effects.

The file we created is on the CD, called Swastika_spice.bmp.

**18.** Using your transition couldn't be easier. Simply apply the SpiceMaster effect to a certain layer and navigate to your new transition. You will need to click the Refresh Folder option on the SpiceMaster control panel to see your new transition take effect.

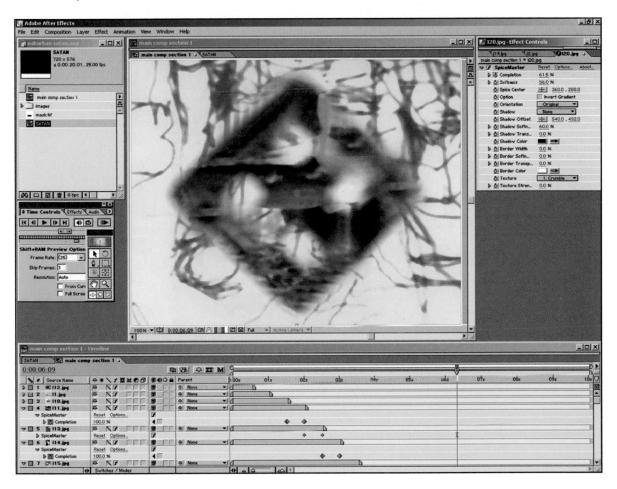

Now, for a slightly different transitional effect, we want to use Delirium's Flow Motion, which pushes all the right buttons when applied to two layers with different shapes and colors – the more diverse, the more interesting the final effect.

**19.** As before, select the next layer you are set to work on, and from the Effect menu, select Delirium > Flow Motion.

**20.** Set keyframes, as for SpiceMaster, with keyframes representing 0% and 100% transition completion.

Again, there are a myriad of options, and you can choose as you see fit how to manipulate them. I have always liked the default settings for this filter, as they always give excellent blends.

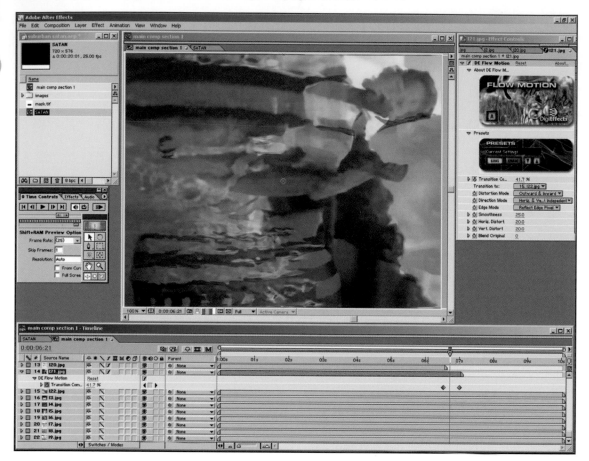

I suggest you mix up a few Flow Motion transitions between some of the remaining transitions that you have to complete in the first section. Another interesting element of Flow Motion is that you don't have to blend to the next layer below, but instead can choose to morph to any layer in the timeline stack.

## Zooming between sections

Now we want to incorporate the stroked symbols and the zooms between layers.

1.  Create a new composition and call it 'final sequence'.

2.  Drag the last composition we created from the project window on to the timeline. You will see a gray bar, which represents all of the layers that we were previously working on.

We are going to begin the strokes, using Maya Paint Effects Stroke On, exactly half way after each section. Given that when you complete the project, you will be shrinking each section by 1 second, the strokes will start progressively faster through each section. We want this stroke to take three quarters of the remaining time, with the final quarter in the section being dedicated to the zoom through the symbol.

3. On the first section, place the timeline head at 5 seconds, and on the comp select Effects > Alias Wavefront > PFX Stroke On.

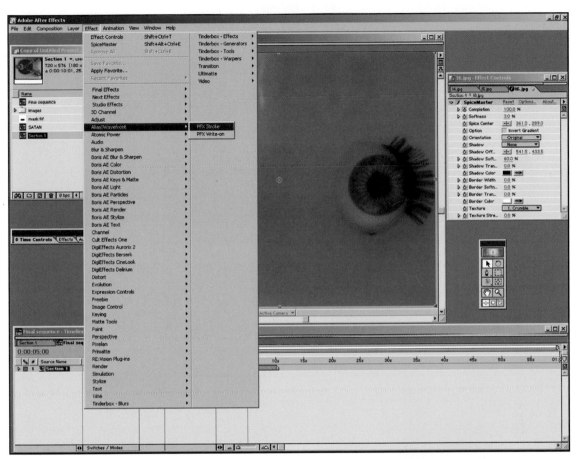

First up, we are going to create the horror classic upside down cross.

4. Double-click on the composition in the timeline, and draw an upturned cross using the pen tools. Be careful not to join the ends, leaving a small gap between them, so that the full image remains on screen unmasked.

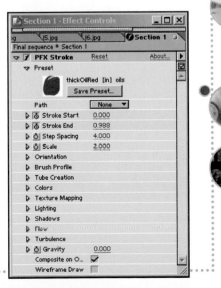

5.  Select thickOilRed from the Oil Presets, as this looks like nice stodgy blood. Set the Scale to 2. Keyframe as explained is step 20. This time, you only need to keyframe either the start or the end positions, depending on whether you want the cross to be drawn clockwise or counterclockwise.

Now things get a little bit tricky, but stick with us.

6.  Re-drag the Section 1 composition from the project box to the timeline, underneath the one we just stroked. Line the start of the composition up with the final keyframe of the Maya Paint Effects filter.

7.  Copy and paste the cross mask, with the unconnected end, onto the composition we just put on the timeline. Close the end of the cross, so that the mask creates a matte.

8.  Apply the same Paint Effects effect in the same way, but make sure that you don't keyframe – just ensure that the entire cross is surrounded by the red pastel, Scale 2.

9.  Now we will animate the shape and scale of the masks, along with Opacity, so that as the red 'blood' finishes on the first comp, the second comp fades up in the middle of the cross and expands to fill the screen.

Phew, this is a complex one, but the end results are worth it! To help with the keyframe settings, as this is very important for this section, we have keyframes at the following positions:

■  On the first composition, now at the bottom of the stack, we have Stroke keyframes at 5 seconds and at 8 seconds.

■  On the comp at the top of the stack, we have Opacity keyframes at 8 seconds and at 9 seconds.

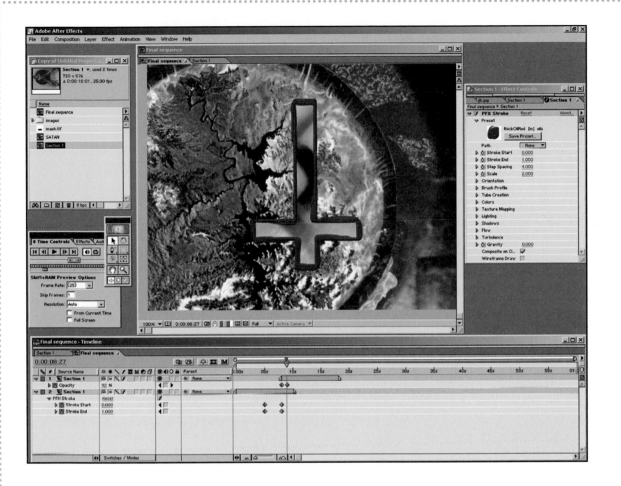

10. On the top comp, press M to get to the mask settings. At 9 seconds and 10 seconds, place keyframes in the Mask Shape option.

11. Double-click on the edge of the mask to activate its Transformation controls. Scale until the cross is too large to be seen on screen. Rotate it 90 degrees as well. To show you how it should look, I have shrunk the screen to 12.5%.

There you go, it wasn't that tricky – was it? We have used two instances of the section 1 comp.

When you download the 'vile' imagery, you will use about 200 images to create a very long, very complex, but excellent looking intro sequence.

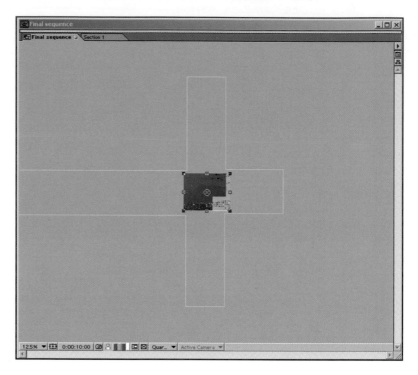

For now, repeat what we have just done, but on subsequent sections create a swastika, a pentagram (not overlapping the edges) or any arcane symbols you fancy. You can check out the ones we used in the After Effects file on the CD and in the finished movie!

## Finishing touches

We will have a black screen and the music fading up for 5 seconds before the previous 1 minute kicks in.

1.  Create another composition, this time called 'All together'. Make it 2 min 0 secs long.

2.  Drag the file `Highland Cattle.wav` to the timeline. Keyframe the volume controls and drag the previous composition to the timeline. Again, this is a nested composition, so everything from the previous composition will be represented by 1 line.

3.  Keyframe Opacity at 3 and 5 seconds, from 0 to 100. Use Easy Ease in from the keyframe assistant and, blow me down with a feather, you've done it!

Render, sit back and relax – this is hard work, but much harder for me, so think yourself lucky!

## Special thanks

Thank you to everyone at Bigmpact TV for putting up with me for the past few years and helping us to make some of the hottest AE work around. A huge thanks to my beautiful wife, Marketa, and everyone at Computer Arts for giving me an outlet for my After Effects and DV ramblings. Here's to many more exciting projects and fun years.

# CHRISTIAN DARKIN

Christian Darkin is a writer, animator and filmmaker. He has written on video editing for dozens of magazines including Computer Arts, Camcorder User, and Digit, as well as the Times, The Guardian and the Financial Times. He's the co-author of two other friends of ED titles, Revolutionary Premiere, and Revolutionary After Effects.

He's written and directed and edited several short films and written two plays for The Edinburgh Festival, comedy sketches for TV and BBC radio, and a video off-shoot of TV series Doctor Who. Current writing projects include a production for a local children's theatre company www.openwidetheatre.co.uk.

His animation work has included effects for several short films as well as more down-to-earth logo animations. He's also created several 2D and 3D animated films including a sci-fi version of Shakespeare's The Tempest.

He's also the author of the Darwin plug-in for 3d studio max - a package designed to allow 3D animators to assemble creatures from a library of body parts (www.digimation.com), and is currently working on another add-on for creating and animating text effects.

The project from which this chapter comes includes a real-time 3D simulation of a prehistoric sea designed for museums which allows visitors to swim with some of the creatures from the same era as the creature featured here. www.geocities.com/christiandarki/fish.htm

# HOW TO RESURRECT A DEAD FISH

Bringing 3D models into and out of reality,
including special Text FX

8

Ichthyophobics look away now...

After Effects has a range of functions for compositing CG effects into shot video. It's also got lots of tools for text animation and other, more graphical jobs. Usually a project will entail one or the other. This one involves both.

Our job is to bring to life an extinct fish from a time before the dinosaurs. The Bothriolepis (both-ree-oh-lee-pis) was a fish from the Devonian period, which evolved strange insect-like legs, instead of fins, protruding from a hard shell covering its whole upper body.

The animation we have to produce is a piece to form part of a multimedia display for a natural history museum. What we're creating is a piece of work which will convince the museum owners that a worthwhile display can be produced, and because we're using After Effects – rather than a much more expensive post-production studio – we hope to produce something high quality, but which the museum can afford. It's a section from a much larger commission we hope to win.

The strange beast needs to be modeled, animated and placed into a real underwater scene. We'll have to composite the scenes to create a realistic set of shots of the creature. The idea of the display is to teach the viewer about evolution, and there's a lot of textual information about the creature that needs to be displayed. We're going to do that by bringing the fish out of the 'real-life' shot into a graphical display where labels, and other information can be presented in an interesting way.

What we have, then, are two kinds of shot, each presenting its own problems, and its own opportunities for creativity. It's always a good move right from the start to think not about what's possible, but about what you want. There are hundreds of ways to get your graphics screen up, and hundreds of styles. Some are very easy, and very flashy – using tools that After Effects provides in a single click.

In our shot we wanted to develop a distinctive style. Not that we wanted to be completely revolutionary in our graphics, or produce something so outlandish that it distracted from the subject of the program. We simply wanted to make our own decisions about what we were trying to achieve and avoid letting the After Effects filters list dictate our style for us.

This outlook leads to more complicated projects, but it generally produces more fulfilling and interesting ones. First come the realistic shots, the scenes of the fish swimming in a primitive ocean. We'll have to texture and light the fish effectively, and animate it realistically. We don't have the budget for an underwater shoot so we're going to have to use stock footage.

## Stock exchange

Stock footage is rarely shot with the needs of the effects designer in mind, and we'll have to overcome some basic problems. The most obvious is camera motion. Scuba divers don't use tripods, so the shots will need to be motion tracked. There also won't be too many good high-contrast stationary points on which to base our motion tracking, so the task won't be an easy one. That said, our fish will be free-swimming and floating around, so some inconsistencies in the tracking will just look like the effect of underwater currents if we handle them correctly.

Our next problem is going to be color balance. We'll need to tune the colors and contrasts in our 3D model to blend in with those of the background, creating a single seamless image in which the fish appears to be a part of the real scene. This is hard enough on land; underwater, light takes on a whole new set of qualities which we'll have to match.

BONY SHIELD    DORSAL FIN
ASYMETRICAL TAIL
**BOTHRIOLEPIS**
30 CM LONG
PELVIC FINS
JOINTED ARMS

Our other shot is a completely different challenge. We have to bring the creature out of its real environment, place it squarely on the screen where the viewer can get a good look at it, x-ray it, and produce labels and other text information to inform the viewer about the fish. Here, reality is not an issue. The fish itself still has to look real, but it doesn't have to blend with its environment. Instead, it has to be placed on a slab and effectively dissected. What will be important here is clarity, and graphical style along with a smooth and unified style of animation for the movement of the creature, its transition into and out of the real world, and the text and graphics which will be placed around it.

Cost, however is an issue, so it's inevitable that our library of underwater stock footage was always – to a certain extent – going to have to define the shots for the real-world part of the project. There's quite a lot of footage about, but most of it is images of certain easily recognizable creatures. After viewing a selection of shots, we'd seen a lot of images of sharks, whales and rays, and a lot of reef shots in which shoals of modern fish make the scene completely unusable.

We toyed with the idea of producing the entire movie in 3D, modeling the plants, corals and other fish needed to make the scenes realistic. This would have made our shots completely controllable, and allowed us to get any composition and angle we wanted. However, we'd have to sacrifice realism. The work involved in creating a realistic environment would have been huge. Particularly difficult would have been the liquid itself. Modeling the thousands of tiny particles floating in the water, and the way the light refracts and reflects through it would have been tough. Getting the complex movement of the currents over the water plants would have been even trickier.

Using a real backdrop not only saves time, it also makes the shot a lot more believable. Eventually, we found what we were looking for – a couple of shots from a diver swimming over the seabed. There was nothing much in the foreground, so our fish could become the subject of the shot, as though the camera was tracking it. The background contained a few indistinct fish, but the shapes could have been contemporaries of Bothriolepis. In addition, we managed to locate a rather lovely sunlight shot – an image looking up through a coral with the sun's rays streaming through. This would allow us to produce an effective silhouette shot if we handled it correctly.

In case you're interested, all the stock footage came from Ulead's 'pick-a-video' footage library. It's a massive library of cheap footage which comes in CD-ROM and DV resolution versions so that it can be easily slotted into any project. Because we'd bought the library, the footage is copyright free, and we can use it in any way we like in our projects (within certain limitations).

## Modeling and animation

Bothriolepis was a fish which died out roughly at the same time as the first amphibians were crawling out of the water. This means that photographs of it are pretty hard to come by. Our 3D model will have to be based on sketches and pictures we find on the Internet and in books, along with an examination of the creature's skeleton. We can make a few assumptions based on images of other fish, but the color of the animal is going to have to be entirely invented.

We've used 3d studio max as our modeling tool. It's got some of the best tools for subdivision surfaces around. However, most 3D applications will offer some similar functions, and even though the methods might differ, the basic tools are pretty universal nowadays. We start very simply. We create a box. We then start to extrude more boxes from it. From the back, we pull out a long rectangle, which we use the Bevel tool to scale down to form a tail. From the front we extend a shorter shape sloping down towards the head. Slowly we build up complexity, adding fins, and refining the shape until we create a very boxy version of what the fish should look like.

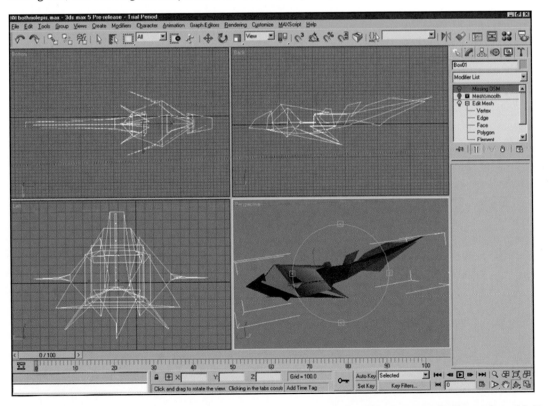

The result might be okay for a videogame, but it's not going to convince anyone in the real world. However, as soon as we add a mesh smoothing modifier (which simply splits each face on the model into a number of new faces, smoothing and blending them together into a more rounded model – other packages have other names for the process, but it's simple enough in most programs), the fish begins to look like a real creature.

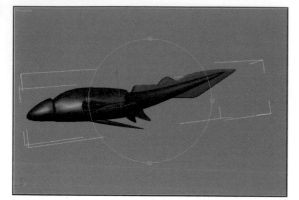

What's really going to sell our shot is the textures we create for the animal. Using a UV unwrapping tool, we unwrap our model, creating a single image in which all the shapes making up the creature are arranged like a sewing pattern. We can paint directly onto this shape, confident in the knowledge of where each stroke will appear on the finished model, and of the fact that there won't be any smearing, or gaps in the texture. This one detail saved us several hours of frustrating work, or about £300 that we'd have to have spent on a stand-alone package to do the job. You can find similar tools in Lightwave and Maya – some of the cheaper packages will be more of a struggle.

The painting itself was done with Deep Paint 3D (www.righthemisphere.com) but we could have used any number of 3D paint packages, or even at a push, a 2D application like Photoshop. As long as we've got the layout map (pictured right) we can see what to paint where.

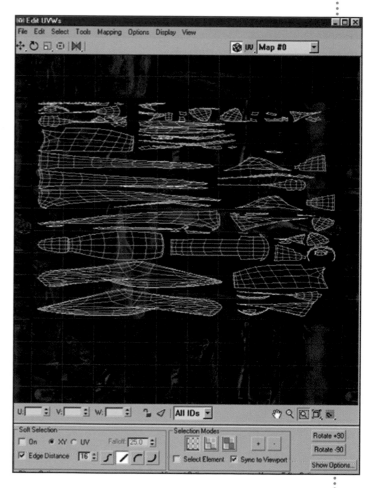

Another tool of some of the newer 3D applications allows us to light our scene not with ordinary lights, but with a spherical projection made out of the stock footage shots we're going to be compositing the creature with. This immediately produces a realistic lighting setup, which will help us tremendously when we get into After Effects. If you can't get this, you'll just have to create a believable lighting setup yourself. This will make color balancing the image a little tougher, but it's still possible.

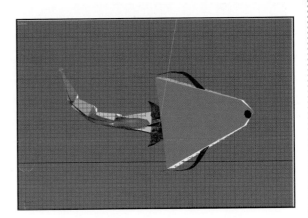

A very quick and easy string of bones let us animate the fish's swimming motion. It's only the movement of the tail from side to side, but we could have created a whole range of different swimming styles for Bothriolepis.

First we experimented with a clumsy, laborious stroke – the head and body twisting from side to side. This gave the impression that the massive bony head and body shield made swimming difficult, and made the creature move like a giant tadpole. Next we tried a stiff-tailed motion – like a tuna – where the force of each movement came from the base of the spine, and the rest of the tail was held straight to give the stroke power. Next up we went for a quivering style, where the fish flapped vigorously for a second or so, then drifted until it sank slowly down, and had to spring into action again. This movement is reminiscent of bottom feeding fish, but didn't seem to suit our creature.

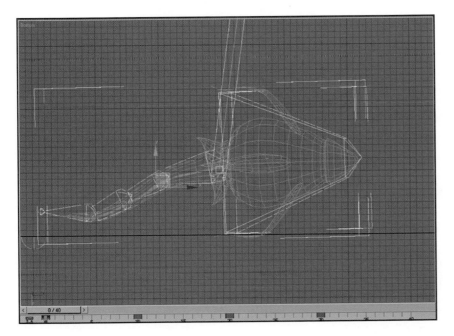

Eventually we plumped for a slow, languid motion, the movement flowing through the body from head to tail. To get this kind of motion, we created just four keyframes for each bone in the tail.

For each shot we imported our stock footage as a backdrop to help us position the fish, and animated the virtual camera to create slight bobbing and drifting motions to add a little randomness to the shot, then we rendered each scene as a sequence of still images. These were rendered with Alpha Channels in place so that the fish would import into After Effects against a transparent background ready to be placed into the shot scene.

## Compositing

Our first shot to get the After Effects treatment was the overhead shot. The footage we began with was very strong. The camera points straight up from the seabed looking right into the sun through the surface of the water. Rays are refracted through the surface ripples, and then filtered by a coral hanging onto a rocky outcrop. It's a lovely scene.

Our creature was rendered as a silhouette, which we could have just placed over the image. However, we wanted to add a little more realism.

We decided the fish would seem more a part of the scene if, as it swam, it broke the rays of light, and cast shadows with them. This added massively to the 3D rendering time (pushing it up from a couple of hours to around 40!). All we did was to add a volume light with a few rays at the center of the screen.

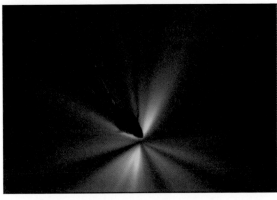

We then imported our CG and shot footage clips into After Effects, and could begin the compositing.

1. With our shot imported as TGAs with alpha channels attached, initial compositing was easy – just drop the two scenes into a new composition and the fish appears in shot.

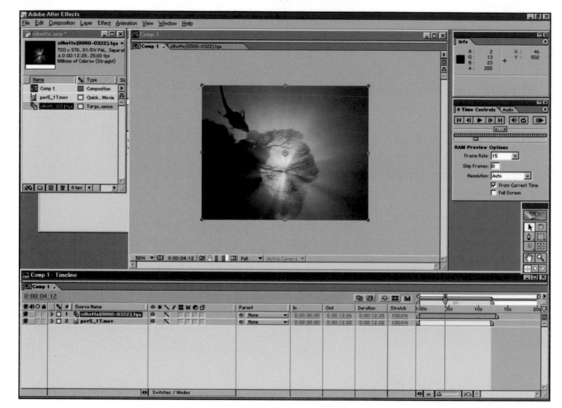

When importing stills into After Effects, the package assumes a frame rate of 30 frames per second, and sometimes ignores your alpha channel. We designed our scene for PAL TV, so it was rendered at 25 fps, and we needed the alpha channel to work so that the fish would composite against our video scene. We initially missed this difference and wondered why our shot suddenly seemed too short, and its background was opaque!

2. It's easy to change After Effects' defaults (by right-clicking (CONTOL-click on the Mac) on the shot in the project window, and selecting Interpret Footage > Main).

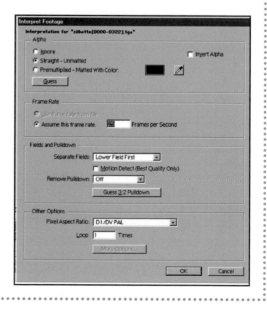

3.  Because it's a silhouette, color matching between the CG and real footage isn't an issue. We did add a Brightness and Contrast filter to slightly lighten the fish footage. This was because most shot footage isn't quite as saturated or high contrast as CG material. The blacks are never quite as black, and the colors are never quite as bright.

4.  The real work was in matching the movement. Obviously, the camera was being held by a scuba diver, so there was a lot of floating about, and this needed to be corrected. We could have handled this by stabilizing the video shot, but it was felt that the scene would be more authentic if we kept the drifting motion, and simply applied it to the fish layer.

5.  Bringing up the Motion Tracker window (Production Bundle version only) we set the tracker to track Position and Rotation. This gives us two linked boxes.

6.  To get the tracking right, we need to position each of these over a non-moving area of high contrast in the shot.

It was quite an easy job. The coral and the rock face provided some very high-contrast points that could be tracked relatively easily. Each track point consists of two boxes – the smaller box contains the section of image to be tracked.

The larger box is the area around the image which After Effects will search in every frame to find the tracked shape. There's not that much motion – if there had been a lot, we'd have had to expand the larger boxes to cover the area moved in each frame. The larger the boxes, the longer the track will take to process, and the more chance there is that the tracker will mistakenly find another similar looking image, and jump to that.

7.  By tracking two points, the package can see not only how the shot is moving laterally, but also how whether it's rotating. With the points positioned, we simply hit Apply, and the scene is processed. This creates the keyframes in the composition.

8.  After Effects isn't too good when it comes to positioning the shot after you've tracked it – you need to place the pivot point. The pivot point of the fish layer defines where the image will be placed, so you need to move the point (not the image itself) after you've tracked the shot. You can't do that while the finished composition updates on the screen, so it's a trial and error job.

If you've got a tricky composite, it's often best to remove the background once you've tracked it, then create a new composition, and drag the motion-tracked composition into that. That way you can position it as though it was a normal layer, without worrying about messing up the tracking (remember, however, that you can mess up the track if you alter the rotation of the shot).

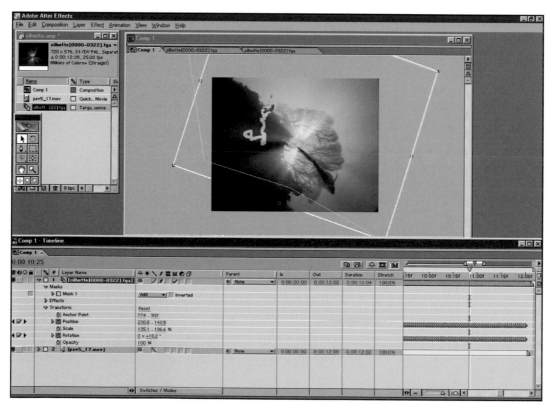

9. With the track done we had to scale the CG portion of the shot up a little, so that when it moved around the screen its edges didn't show.

10. In fact there was a point at which the bottom edge was visible (only by the fact that the rays of light ended abruptly at the corner). We could have expanded the shot even more to overlap the edge, but the image would have become less sharp. Instead, we solved this by drawing a simple mask around the whole image.

11. We then used the Mask Feather tool to soften the edges until they were unnoticeable, so that the rays faded out gently towards the edge of the screen.

12. Rendering the finished shot, it looked impressive. With hindsight, it would have been better to have rendered the light rays and the fish as separate layers so that we could have varied the opacity of the rays independently of the fish to tune the image more easily. With better planning, we'd have covered this, However, the effect is still a powerful image and it is very convincing.

## Swimming with the fishes

Next up came the 'fish following' shot. The stock footage was of the seabed, and the camera operator had taken it by swimming just above the bottom, looking forward and slightly down. The result was a long, slow track over the coral, with an empty foreground perfect for compositing our fish into. The shot would look as though we were swimming with the ancient placoderm, following it across the seabed.

**13.** Rendering the 3D shot was pretty straightforward. The camera was placed behind the fish, and moved towards and away from it just a little to simulate drifting with the current. The rest of the motion would be added in After Effects.

**14.** Compositing the two shots, we realized that color correction was going to be a little trickier than in the last scene. We'd done our best in the 3D application, but fine-tuning would still be necessary. The Color Balance and Brightness and Contrast filters (both under Effect > Adjust) were added to pull the two scenes together.

Other compositors (combustion particularly) have stronger color balance tools, but we chose After Effects anyway because we have a whole range of requirements for this project. The Color Balance tool allows us to adjust the red, green, and blue levels in the shadows, midtones, and highlights of the image, and this was pretty vital in getting the right kind of lighting for our underwater world.

**15.** Trial and error is often the best approach to color balance. However, if you start by getting the level of black and white right, then begin to alter your object's colors until they are similar the other objects in the scene and you'll be half way there.

Underwater, reds and purples are the first things to fade as blue light becomes dominant, so we're not concerned with keeping the model's original color. Even the brightest object would appear greenish blue down here.

The result looked okay, but we decided to add to it with a little blurring of the super-sharp CG fish.

**16.** We also add a noise filter to add grain (our underwater shot would have been taken in dark conditions, so there was more video noise than in a well exposed dry-land shot).

Noise has to be handled subtly – we don't want to make the image too fuzzy. We just give it a small amount of noise. Even with all this, the composite was not perfect, so we decided to cheat.

**17.** Once the shot was finished, we created a new composition and dragged the old one into it. We then added a CineLook filter to it, adding more grain and color correction to make the shot look as though it was shot on film. CineLook (www.digieffects.com) is a third party add-on for After Effects, and is a useful tool to have around for altering the quality of a scene.

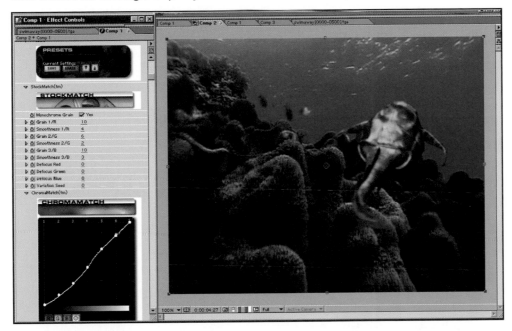

If you've been unable to do a really good color matching job in a composite, it's often a good idea to add a final color or brightness tweak to the whole scene. Because you're adjusting the CG and shot footage in the same way, the two parts of the image are smoothed together and the final shot appears more integrated. There's a trade-off here – the more detail you remove in order to minimize the visibility of your errors, the worse the quality of your shot is going to be.

Motion tracking was also going to be a problem. After Effects can only motion track in 2D, across the screen and up and down it. Motion in our shot was definitely 3D – the camera was floating over the coral, so even if we could get a point to track (which we couldn't as nothing remained in shot throughout the entire scene) it wouldn't have worked because the main movement was towards the camera.

18. In the end we went for a random motion for the fish, created with the Motion Sketch tool (Window > Motion Sketch). This lets you capture the motion of the mouse, and apply it to the position of a layer on screen. It enables you to produce natural looking motion, but because it captures a keyframe for every frame, the movement can be quite jerky.

19. The way around that is to use The Smoother (Window > The Smoother). Simply select all the keyframes, then Apply. This attempts to keep the basic shape of our motion, but removes most of the keyframes, creating a much less jerky movement. We have to apply The Smoother a few times, or change the Tolerance, to get the best result.

The finished shot is frankly not the best effect ever produced. The fish and the camera aren't exactly in sync. The effect is saved by the fact that it's underwater, and the fish and camera are both moving quickly. In addition, the fish isn't in contact with any object in the scene so there's nothing for the eye to compare its movement with. We've also made sure the shot was long enough that we can pick and choose the best few seconds for our final sequence. There's a slightly unrealistic drifting motion, but it's the best we can do in the circumstances.

## Abandoning the real world

Our most challenging After Effects job in the entire project was to take the fish out of its environment, place it onto a graphical screen, dissect it, label all its unique features, and then finally re-assemble it and put it back into the water.

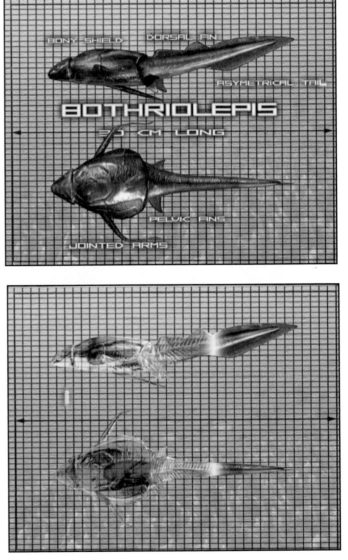

This 30 second long sequence required a whole range of techniques and skills, and took longer than any other part of the process. In the end we used dozens of layers in After Effects, several pre-compositions, three external programs, and a whole range of tricks and cover-ups to achieve the required shot. We also used the Glow filter on no less than 23 occasions.

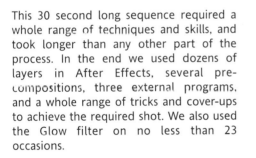

We decided that the style of the effect would be a little like a character page in a video game – the fish would be shown in two elevations, from the side and from the top. It would be placed on a technical-drawing style grid, and the labels and text would teletype themselves onto the screen. The fish needed to become transparent so that its bone structure could be seen, and we decided this would be achieved with a kind of glowing scan line which sliced away the screen, leaving a transparent version behind it.

As always, preparation is the most important part of the job. If we've got all the shots we're going to need for the composite, the finished scene will be assured.

20. We start with the original scene from which the creature will be plucked. It's an easy composite, and once we'd done the other two shots above, it was simple to produce a shot of the fish swimming across a relatively stationary coral reef.

21. The motion tracker is brought into play, but it's an easy track as the camera's motion is gentle, and we don't track into or out of the shot. We only track position – not rotation as we did last time – so the track is a simple one to do.

22. Color correction is also pretty easy. Once we'd done the previous shot, we knew what we were looking for, and we just had to increase the blues and greens in the image.

23. To make sure the creature moved completely through the shot, we also added lateral movement, so the fish would begin off screen to the left, and end up off screen to the right.

**24.** Next up we need the grid — an illustration package allowed us to quickly put that together, and Photoshop provided it with a nice papery texture.

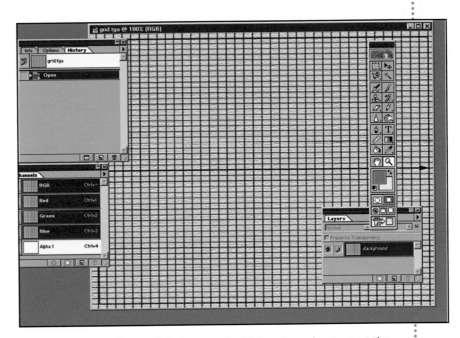

**25.** Next comes the fish animation. We export the frame of our original scene at which we're going to start the shot, and we use it as a backdrop in 3ds max.

**26.** We then position the fish exactly over the fish in the rendered scene and create a new animation with it.

In this, the fish simply spins out at us, placing itself in the top third of the screen in a side view. It then spins downwards to end up in the bottom third in profile. We'll need three things from this shot: the animation itself, the final frame, and the middle frame where the creature is in its side view.

**27.** We render the animation with Motion Blur, but turn it off for the two still shots.

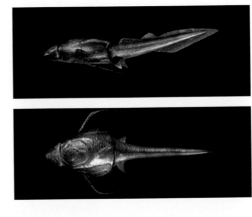

**28.** Finally, we'll need two more renders of the fish in the two final positions (side on and top down). This time, we change the material the model is made from into a kind of glass, and place behind it an image of the grid we created as our background.

**29.** Using Photoshop, we add a couple of extra images of skeletons – there's no way round this I'm afraid you've basically got to draw them. We turn these last two pictures into x-ray versions of the fish. This is a tricky job, but we use the clone tool to produce our effect, and alter the overlay mode for a more translucent effect.

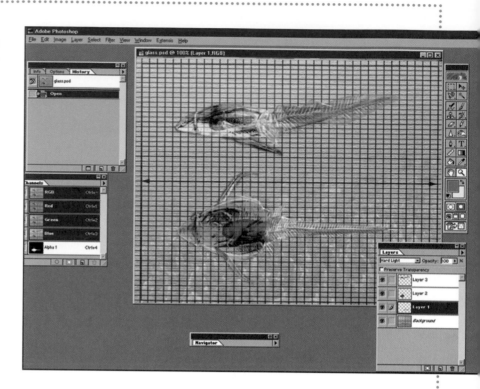

## Textuallity

The final job before we start putting everything together was to create animations for the text which has to appear on-screen. Here again, we have to think about style. Because of the video game look we want to create, we're going to go for a modern typeface, and have it written onto the screen as though it's being typed, but with each letter glowing as it hits the screen – as though it's being burnt into a cathode ray tube.

We tried a number of methods. None was particularly good, and most were overcomplicated. Writing words onto the screen is something which gets done so often that writers of titling packages often include it as a standard effect. However we want a greater degree of control, and need to be able to make the currently typing letter glow, so none of these was really suitable.

1. In After Effects, we create a new composition and a solid, onto which we type our text.

2. We then create another black solid right on top, set this as an Alpha Inverted Matte for the type layer. You may need to click the Switches/Modes button at the bottom of the timeline to get access to the matte controls (which are a pull-down under the TrkMat heading).

3. The effect of this is that where the solid covers the text, the text is visible, and where the solid doesn't overlap, the text vanishes. Animating the solid across the screen, the text is made to reveal itself as though it's being typed in.

The key here is that, because the solid is being used as an Alpha Matte, it's transparent, so when we come to add our text effect to the rest of our composite, its background will vanish, and we can place it wherever we like on screen and the effect will be the same.

4. Next we produce another solid – this time a tiny one – about the size of a single letter. Make it white, and apply a Glow filter (Effect > Stylize > Glow) to its alpha channel, producing a glowing white blob.

5. Placing this at the left-hand edge of the solid we're using as a mask, make the mask layer its parent. Now, as the text reveals itself, we've got a glowing cursor preceding it.

The Glow filter is available only in the Production Bundle version of After Effects. If you don't have it, you can try using a gentle blur along with a brightness filter to replicate the effect. It's not a perfect solution, but can be effective.

6. We don't want the cursor as a block, we want it as a glowing letter, so duplicate the text layer, and place the copy on top of the glowing blob layer.

7. Then set this copy as the Alpha Matte of the blob layer. Now, the blob is only seen through the text, so you just get a glowing letter.

**8.** It looks pretty good, but for a final little touch we add a Glow to our masking text layer. This slightly blurs the letter-shaped stencil, and allows the glow from the blob to slightly overlap the edges of the text for a slightly fuzzier, less harsh glowing letter.

You'll need to experiment to get a level of glow you like for each part of the effect. In this case the Glow Threshold setting doesn't matter much because everything's only one color, but the Radius and Intensity need to be set. You can change the color easily too, with controls on the filter's control panel.

We could have simply imported copies of this project into our final After Effects composite, but with seven different text layers, and each of these containing all the above layers and effects, our project would have become very slow and complex.

**9.** Instead, render out each line of text as a separate image sequence (TGA images with transparent backgrounds for easy compositing). The text items need to be rendered big enough to fill the screen – remember they can be resized when we import them into our finished scene.

## Out of reality

Time to start work on the main feature.

**30.** Import a still from the backdrop from which the swimming creature will spin into our graphical display (the still of the frame at which the action will be frozen for the shot), and the 3D animation of it spinning out, – and we're ready to begin.

The swimming fish has been color balanced for the environment it's in, whereas the new shot of the fish has been rendered with uniform lighting for the graphical display. They don't match. This problem could be solved in a number of ways. We could go back and look at the color correction settings we'd applied to our first animation, and then blend them out as the fish spins into place. It's an elegant solution, and would create a smooth change between the two shots.

However, we don't want a smooth change – this is an unreal effect. We decided to apply a bold glow to the fish. The strength of the glow is animated from a full white flash to nothing in just under half a second so that the fish appears to flash as it starts moving, as though it was being pulled out of reality by some technological means.

**31.** We place the glow and turn on animation only for its function. The intensity animation makes the glow brighter and dimmer. The glow is set to affect the alpha channel, so that it appears around the fish. If it was set to color channels, it would affect the brightest parts of the fish.

**32.** As the fish reaches its first position – the profile shot in the top third of the screen – we do two things. First, we add another glowing flash. This is pretty much a copy of the first.

**33.** Second, we import a still frame of the fish in this position, and place it on top (with a corresponding glow of its own).

**34.** When it reaches its final position, we do the same again.

Now the fish is spinning out, leaving a copy of itself in profile, and then rotating down to flash again, and coming to rest as a top view at the bottom of the screen.

**35.** Time to bring in the grid, and with a two keyframe animation we slide it in between the fish and its backdrop, giving it a slight transparency so you can still just see the seabed behind.

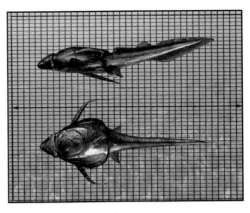

The effect is coming on very nicely. A quick preview render confirms this. We've gone from a realistic shot to a graphical screen seamlessly in about 2 seconds, and the effect is pleasing.

Next we have to go from the 2 elevations of the model to the skinned versions we created in Photoshop. Again, there is a good range of ways to do this. The easiest is a simple opacity animation, fading one shot into the other. However, we're not into doing things the easy way, we want a more digital, and at the same time more medical looking process. The idea is to use a vertical glowing scan line which sears across the image, removing the skin.

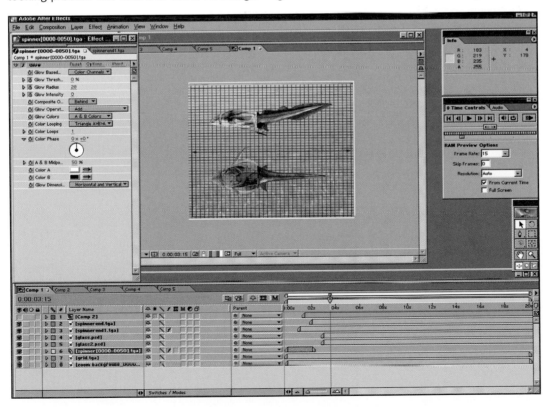

**36.** The first step is simple enough. We lay the two glass fish underneath the original ones, and draw a simple square mask on the top layer. This covers the entire screen.

**37.** Then we animate the mask to scroll across, wiping off the layers containing the original render. Easy.

**38.** Now we're going to use a method similar to the one with which we created our glowing letters. Create a long thin solid, and give it a Glow filter. A copy of our two transparent fish is used as an Alpha Matte so that the glow only appears within their outline.

We can't parent the strip to the movement which reveals the fish as it's a mask this time and not a layer, so we have to animate it separately. It's not too difficult as long as the bar isn't too narrow, because you don't have to be very precise. In any case, the mask only has two keyframes, so its motion is smooth.

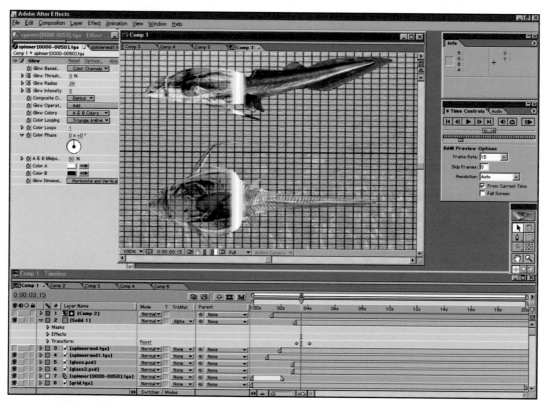

## Write on

Okay, the fish are in place, and stripped down. The writing needs to be placed in. We've rendered each piece of text as a full screen so that it can be positioned now.

**39.** We import each text animation twice – once as an animation, and once as a single frame (the final frame in the animation where all the text has been revealed).

Our project is beginning to look overcomplicated, so it's helpful to start a new composition, dragging the old one into it. This doesn't change the scene at all, it just means that instead of looking at a timeline with 9 layers each with its own animation and settings, we only need to look at one layer – the finished backdrop.

This makes everything clearer for us, and means the project will be easier to follow if anyone else needs to work on it.

40. Onto our new composition – we drag the first text animation.

41. We then immediately drag the final frame on top, placing it in time so that the still appears exactly as the animation is completed. We make one layer a parent of the other using the parenting controls on the timeline.

42. We need to do the same with each piece of text, positioning them in time, so that the captions appear one at a time, and are placed correctly on the screen.

## Backtracking

Okay, we're half way there. Now everything needs to go back. The text has to vanish, the backdrop has to slide away, and the fish has to be released back into the wild. We want the rest of our effect to have the same style as the first half, but we don't want it to be the same, so we're going to have to use some other techniques to complete the shot.

Our concept for the ending is that the text – which currently stands out strongly from the backdrop – will set itself into the grid pattern. It will sink back to look as though it's been written onto the paper. With this done, it'll be a lot more natural when instead of vanishing, the text slides out with the grid to reveal the underwater scene behind. The fish can then re-skin itself, join back up as one object, and replace itself where it originally came from. Then we can simply re-start the background shot, and the fish will be seen to swim away.

That was the concept. However, in the final event, the order of things had to change slightly. Although it was entirely possible to do everything as above, we'd have had to do a lot of extra work and a new 3D animation for a certain part of it, and the result really wouldn't have added anything. In design, you can easily become so rigid about your initial ideas that you don't take notice of more interesting or creative ways of doing things when they present themselves, and you can end up creating extra work for yourself without actually improving the finished result. In the end, we made a trivial change, and the whole process became a lot easier. A big part of any creative job is knowing the difference between avoiding wasting your time and energy on pointless obsessions, and compromising your work by cutting corners, but more of that later...

For now, we just want to make the text sink into the background. We take our project and simply turn off the background layer. Remember, before we started with the text, we began a new composition and dragged all the backgrounds, the grid, the fish, and all the animations associated with them in as a single composition. On top of this we laid all the text animations.

43. Turn the background's visibility off, leaving just the text against a transparent backdrop. We now render this out as a still image.

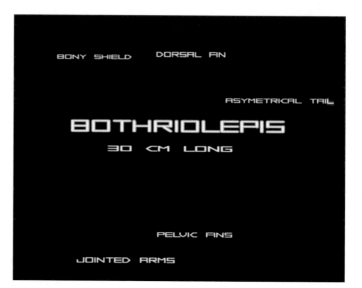

**44.** Our project is already overcrowded with layers, so it will help to start with a blank canvas. Onto this, we drop the background image of the seabed, the grid image (adjusted to the same opacity as before), the x-rayed fish, and finally the text image we've just rendered.

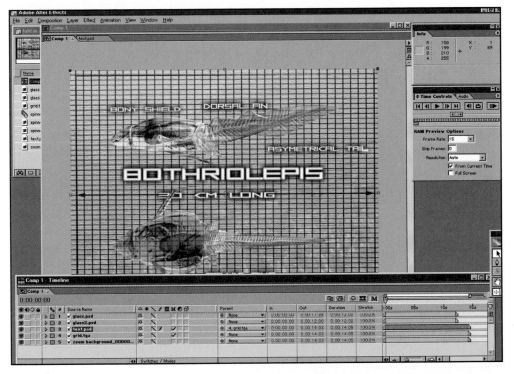

**45.** The shot looks just as it did at the end of the last animation. However, there's one difference: now the text is a single layer which we can fade in and out at will. We animate its Opacity down to about 60%, and it fades to become part of the background.

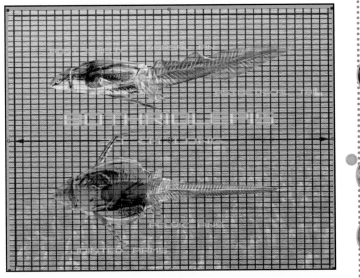

**46.** We then make the grid the parent of the text layer. Now when we animate the grid sliding out, the text moves with it. Put together, it's a surprisingly pleasing effect, considering we've done so little work to achieve it, and we're just about to start feeling smug when we realize why our master plan simply isn't going to work...

The x-ray fish have been rendered as a glass material against the backdrop of the grid. This produced a nice series of reflections and refractions, and made the whole transparent fish graphic look great. However, when we slide the backdrop out, you can still see the grid through the fish, it doesn't move, and you certainly don't get the changing reflections as it passes under them – they're only still images after all.

To solve this, we'd have to go back, and re-render the fish in our 3D package with the grid sliding out from under them at exactly the same speed it was moving in the After Effects shot, and replace the bones of the fish in every frame. We decided to take the easy way out. All we really needed to do was re-skin the fish before the backdrop started to move.

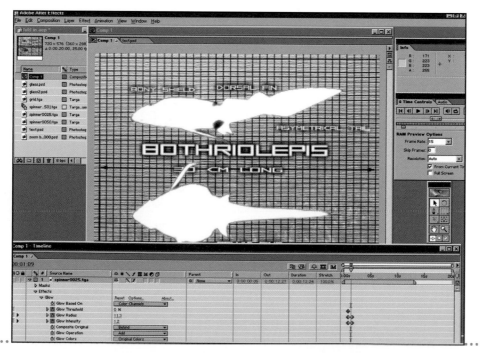

The scanning line we created earlier to skin the fish was appropriate at the time. It led the eye across the shape and attracted the attention to what was going on. It was there to provide interest and to make the viewer ask questions which would be answered by the text captions which were about to appear. Now, however, that is all done, and all that matters is that we get quickly and elegantly back into the water. Bringing the scan line back would just look laborious and over complex.

47. Instead, we just use a flash – created with the Glow filter – lasting about a fifth of a second. As the glow fades, we take the Opacity of the x-rayed fish down to nothing and reveal the skinned layer underneath.

48. We select and drag the keyframes for all this animation and place them just after the text has faded, but before we animate the grid off screen.

49. We're now left with the top and side views of the fish, against a still of the seabed. We put in another flash for the bottom fish, then place the original animation in which the fish spins out of the scene into our graphics shot onto the top layer.

**50.** We play this backwards (by altering the Time Stretch factor to −100%), and the fish spins back into place.

**51.** Finally, we put in one final flash, to cover the transition between the fish we've lit especially for our graphics shot and the one color balanced for the sea scene, and render the effect. Again, we create a still image sequence to preserve quality, although transparency is no longer an issue, so we could simply render it as a QuickTime video file).

We're ready for the moment of truth. We have to assemble all our scenes into a final piece ready to be shown to the client. We could do this in After Effects, but there's no good reason to. This is a job for a video editor. We are using Premiere.

## Putting it all together

We import our three scenes, and start editing. We want to create a relaxed feeling to the whole scene so we've produced relatively long slow sequences. We start with a couple of shots flying over the sea. What we produce here is what you can see in the finished movie on the CD. We won't talk in as great a detail about this as maybe we'd like. Although video editing can be achieved within After Effects it is a composition tool and a dedicated video editor will always beat it for flexibility and ease of use when compiling a set of shots in this manner. This section falls slightly outside the scope of our discussion, but is included for reasons of completeness.

A voice-over will be provided later on, but for now, we just drop in some orchestral music (royalty free music is provided with Premiere, and it's okay for demonstration purposes, but some of it can be too recognizable to be used in real projects).

This sets the mood for the piece, and we gradually mix to a shot of the seabed. Another mix and we bring in our first effects shot. It's the camera following the creature across the seabed. We mix again to the silhouette scene, and again back to a later section of the previous shot.

Next we mix to the first part of our graphics shot. The fish swims in. As it reaches the frame in which our effect begins, we cut to the effect we've created. The effect ends and we cut back – the action appears to continue from where it left off. The result is completely seamless. A success!

Finally, as the fish swims out of shot, we mix back to the first shot of the camera flying over the sea. This project is part of a project for a museum, which we want to play constantly, so it needs to loop.

The images are complete, but that's not the end of the story. Effects are often created or destroyed not by the shot itself, but by the sounds which accompany it. We've got a lot going on in our scene, but underwater you wouldn't really hear any of it.

We blatantly ignore this fact, and place in a range of swishing, and bubbling sounds to create an underwater soundscape. It's common practice for nature programs to put in noise which would never be heard in real life. Think about it – a shot of a pride of lions at a kill has to be shot with a very long lens from a safe distance. How is anybody going to record real sound at that range?

Our graphical scene requires a completely different approach. We used electronic noises, plenty of which are available online and from effects generators and synthesizers if you want them.

A render out from Premiere at the required quality (in our case PAL) and the project Is ready for us to show to our clients. I'd like to tell you about that meeting, but it hasn't happened yet! Hopefully we'll get the commission, and the real work will start...

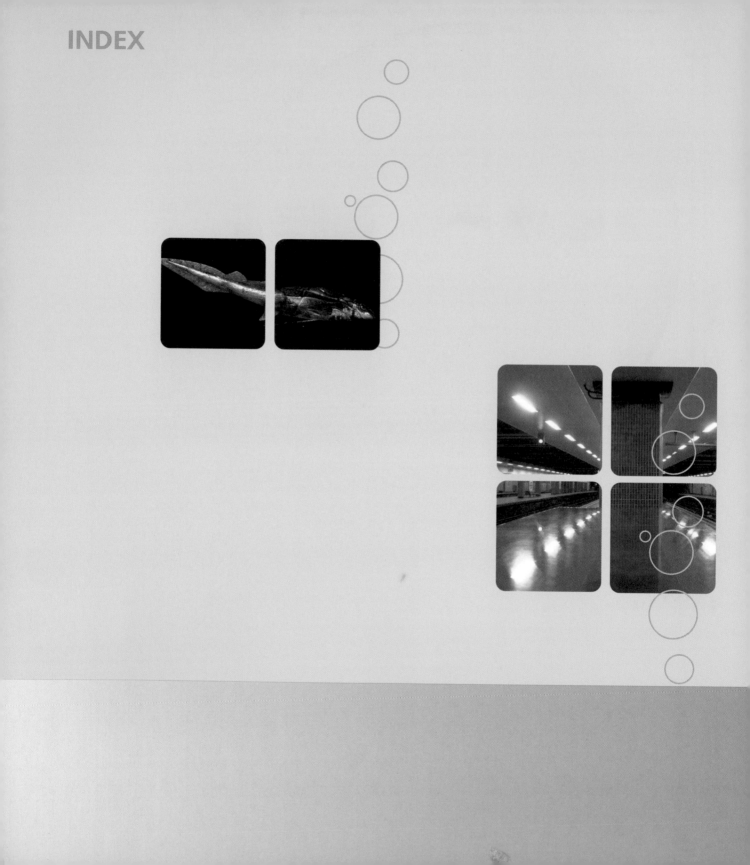

# INDEX

The index is arranged hierarchically, in alphabetical order, with symbols preceding the letter A. Many second-level entries also occur as first-level entries. This is to ensure that users will find the information they require however they choose to search for it.

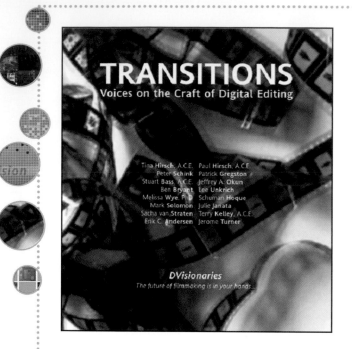

The wisdom of veteran film editors and the vision of digital pioneers are married in this stunning new book. Transitions is the ultimate resource for anyone who has learned the tool and wants to learn the technique, the art and the craft from the best.

Featuring an interview with Paul Hirsch, A.C.E., Oscar-winning film editor of Star Wars (1977) and a chapter by LEE UNKRICH - editor of Toy Story and co-director of the smash hit Monsters, Inc.

Foreword by TINA HIRSCH, A.C.E., president of American Cinema Editors (ACE).

The future of filmmaking is in your hands...

Transitions is a digital editing book like no other. The concept is simple. We take 15 of the very best artists in the film editing field, and we let them teach you, one-to-one, the principles, techniques and lessons that have defined their careers.

There is a great deal to being an editor. From the tricky decision of which cut to make first and the intricacies of building narrative, to the specifics of editing in genres, Transitions aims to capture the life and art of the editor, showing their overlap, indulging their differences, engaging in every author's unique experience and tapping into their hard-gotten wisdom.

Fifteen essays cover diverse subjects from editing animation to weaving multiple storylines, but the focus is always on the art. Whatever your digital editing tool, be it Final Cut Pro, Avid or Adobe Premiere, or even if you are just enthused by film editing, Transitions gives you the blinding art and the sheer craft of modern editing techniques.

The final cut is only the beginning.

The latest release of Adobe's comprehensive compositing and visual effects tool offers an unparalleled range of special effects options to the digital video maker. With new 3D tools, brand new effects and increased productivity and workflow management, After Effects 5.5 is the last word in creating stunning visual experiences for video, film and the web.

Revolutionary After Effects 5.5 brings you everything that this new version has to offer, both Standard Version and Production Bundle and will teach you everything you need to have sheer digital beauty, on your desktop, in the palm of your hand.

Whatever your level, DVision books deliver the core skills, advanced techniques and real-world case studies to send your digital video projects sky-high. Revolutionary After Effects 5.5 covers all you need to know, before you need to know it, backing up every piece of theory with solid practical tutorial.

The focus is on tutorials and how to create effects rather than lengthy descriptions of individual tools. The majority of requests that Al and Colin receive are about producing stunning images, not explaining the tools, so that's what they've concentrated on. We've kept one thing in mind during the making of this book: what do our readers really want?

Al and Colin found they didn't have the space or time on their sites (actionfx.com and PhotoshopCafe.com) to pass on all their knowledge to visitors - people kept asking them for more, more, more... so here it is: more information, more effects, more tips... and lots more!

Photoshop has helped to create an army of devoted followers, not by being relatively easy to pick up, but by having a huge range of creative options available to you once you have learned the basics. You can then let your imagination run wild...

With Foreword by Scott Kelby:

"One of the most powerful features of Photoshop, may be the effect it has on the people who use it. People who use Photoshop are hungry for information, they're hungry to learn the latest tricks, the hot new techniques, and that common interest has an amazing way of bringing like-minded people together."

As with all Friends of ED books, we offer efficient, comprehensive email support absolutely free.

The best, most requested effects that you've seen on the Web and elsewhere, explained by two Photoshop Experts: Al Ward and Colin Smith. In response to feedback from their popular web sites and magazine articles, Al and Colin have teamed up with friends of ED to answer your questions. They've packed in lots of useful information, not just how to create a certain effect, but other tips too, like how to improve your workflow, variations on effects, and creative suggestions to help you express yourself further.

This book is for both the enthusiastic amateur and experienced pro alike - it's full of techniques and advice that will help Photoshop users from intermediate to advanced. This book will help you to stock up your armoury; you'll have a range of weapons for all occasions and be able to deploy them faster and more effectively.

The book is divided into three main sections; the first two are Al and Colin working individually to create the most wanted effects, and in the third section, Al and Colin combine their skills in three different design projects. These projects were selected to demonstrate how designers tackle a variety of tasks when working with others; the questions and issues that may arise, and how the final product is achieved.

DESIGNER TO DESIGNER™

friends of ED writes books for you. Any suggestions, or ideas about how you want information given in your ideal book will be studied by our team.Your comments are always valued at friends of ED.

For technical support please contact support@friendsofed.com.

Free phone in USA: 800.873.9769
Fax: 312.893.8001

UK Telephone: 0121.258.8858
Fax: 0121.258.8868

Registration Code : [                    ]

## After Effects Most Wanted – Registration Card

Name ...........................................................................................

Address .......................................................................................

City .................................................State/Region ...................................

Country ..................................................Postcode/Zip ...............................

E-mail ..........................................................................................

Profession: design student ☐ freelance designer ☐
part of an agency☐ inhouse designer ☐
other (please specify) ...................................

Age: Under 20 ☐ 20-25 ☐ 25-30 ☐ 30-40 ☐ over 40 ☐

Do you use: mac ☐ pc ☐ both ☐

How did you hear about this book?.............................................

☐ Book review (name)...............................................................

☐ Advertisement (name) ..........................................................

☐ Recommendation ..................................................................

☐ Catalog ..................................................................................

☐ Other .....................................................................................

Where did you buy this book? ....................................................

☐ Bookstore (name) ................................City...........................

☐ Computer Store (name).........................................................

☐ Mail Order..............................................................................

☐ Other......................................................................................

How did you rate the overall content of this book?

Excellent ☐ Good ☐

Average ☐ Poor ☐

What applications/technologies do you intend to learn in the near future?.........................................................................

.........................................................................................

What did you find most useful about this book? ...........................

What did you find the least useful about this book? .....................

.........................................................................................

Please add any additional comments ..........................................

.........................................................................................

What other subjects will you buy a computer book on soon?

.........................................................................................

What is the best computer book you have used this year?

.........................................................................................

*Note: This information will only be used to keep you updated about new friends of ED titles and will not be used for any other purpose or passed to any other third party.*

**ISBN** 1-904344-02-X

**friendsof**

DESIGNER TO DESIGNER™

N.B. If you post the bounce back card below in the UK, please send it to:

friends of ED Ltd.,
30 Lincoln Road, Olton,
Birmingham, B27 6PA. UK.

---

NO POSTAGE
NECESSARY
IF MAILED
IN THE
UNITED STATES

# BUSINESS REPLY MAIL

*FIRST CLASS MAIL     PERMIT\*64     CHICAGO,IL*

POSTAGE WIIL BE PAID BY ADDRESSEE

**friends of ED.**
**29 S. LA SALLE ST.**
**SUITE 520**
**CHICAGO IL 60603-USA**